Consumer Insights-
Love them and leverage them

Consumer Insights –
Love them and leverage them

.. und Ihre Marketingaktivitäten werden effektiver

Mel Schoen

Bibliografische Information der Deutschen Bibliothek:

Die Deutsche Bibliothek verzeichnet diese Publikation in der Deutschen
Nationalbibliografie; detaillierte bibliografische Daten sind im Internet über
<http://dnb.ddb.de> abrufbar

©Juni 2006 Mel Schoen
Kontakt: melschoen@insightdriven.de

Cover design: Ottmar Meier, Hamburg
www.werbemeierei.de

Herstellung und Verlag: Books on Demand GmbH, Norderstedt

Printed in Germany

ISBN 3-8334-5182-3

Why you should read this book

Everyone in business dreams of being at the forefront of a famous success. Who wouldn't want to be able to claim that they were part of the team directly responsible for thinking up the iPod, establishing Starbucks or inventing eBay and have the bank balance to prove it?

Well, as such strokes of genius happen so rarely, it is close to a mathematical certainty that this is not going to happen for you or me! So what should those of us in business who are ambitious but realistic be aiming for? My answer would be to ensure we are among the most successful at whatever we do.

Business does not reward doing things well. It rewards doing things better than others, almost regardless of how well anyone is performing objectively. Every race has a winner, every chart has someone at the top and as the old joke says, if you and an acquaintance are running away from a lion you don't have to be faster than the lion....

This book is all about an approach to marketing brands that guarantees a place either at the top or very close to it. Leveraging Consumer Insights whenever possible has little to do with strokes of genius and a lot to do with common sense. It involves applying consistently a stringent way of thinking to brands, knowing that it will work well almost every time. And knowing full well, too, that part of the reason it will work is because most of the competition is not listening to its customers as closely.

I cannot claim, unfortunately, to have invented this approach but I can immodestly say that I am pretty good at applying it. It helps to be totally convinced that leveraging insights is the only sure method of building brands for those of us who are not prone to sudden, life-changing flashes of brilliance.

Looking at the subject from various angles, the book draws on both my own experience of working with a large number of companies and brands in the advertising business for many years and the valuable input that others have provided – knowingly or not.

The book does follow a certain order but it is equally possible, perhaps even advisable, to scan the Contents page and cherry-pick anything that seems interesting. The parts add up to a whole, whatever order they are read in.

Liberal use is made of quoted statements, although most of them are not, to be honest, 100% verbatim. Nonetheless, they are authentic versions of opinions and insights, collected over the years and filed away for future use. It's just that they've been compacted and moulded a little to make their point!

Having read this book you should, at least, be keen to find out what a ruthless approach to leveraging insights could do for you and your brands. Hopefully, having then tried it you, too, will be convinced that anyone who is both ambitious and realistic would be wise to do the same.

Like anyone else in business, I can't guarantee complete success – but I can guarantee that you won't be eaten by the lion.

Mel Schoen

Contents

Consumer Insights – leveraging them............53

Consumer Insights – learning from them.....75

Foreword

- bevor es auf Englisch weitergeht

Wer bietet mehr als 80% Deutsch?

Vor vielen Jahren musste ich eine wichtige New Business Präsentation für die Firma Henkel vorbereiten. Bis dahin hatte ich Präsentationen fast immer nur auf Englisch geschrieben und präsentiert, weil ich nur für internationale Kunden gearbeitet hatte. „Pass bloß auf", riet mir ein Kollege, „diese Firma ist stolz auf ihre Marketingkompetenz und man mag dort keine Anglizismen."

Also habe ich mich bemüht, Fremdwörter auf meinen Folien zu vermeiden und habe beim Präsentieren darauf geachtet, keine Begriffe wie „Benefit", „Image" oder „Advantage" zu verwenden.

Ich habe es auch geschafft, bei der deutschen Marketingsprache zu bleiben und die Präsentation lief gut genug, um mit einem Projektauftrag herauszukommen. Hinterher hatte ich die Chance, mit dem Marketing Direktor unter vier Augen zu sprechen. „Das hat mir gut gefallen", sagte er, „aber es ist mir aufgefallen, dass Sie als Engländer jede Anstrengung unternommen haben, Ihre Muttersprache zu vermeiden. Das war aber gar nicht nötig. Wir reden auch hier über ‚Strategies' und ‚Brand Character'. Es ist sonst viel zu umständlich – wie Sie es gerade selbst erfahren haben."

Seitdem achte ich besonders auf die Sprache, die in Meetings und Präsentationen verwendet wird. Die Marketingsprache war immer Englisch und die deutschen Adaptionen der Begriffe sind unterschiedlich gut gelungen. In einigen neueren Bereichen wie Online-Kommunikation, Mobile Marketing usw. gibt es sogar gar keine gebräuchlichen deutschen Ausdrücke.

Heute ist jedes Marketinggespräch zu einer Art Pingpong-Spiel zwischen den beiden Sprachen geworden. Alle hoffen auch, dass die Fremdworte, die sie selbst benutzen, vom Gesprächspartner genauso verstanden werden. Manchmal werden solche Begriffe sogar völlig falsch benutzt – neulich hörte ich: „Wir haben zusammen gesessen und ein Common Sense erreicht – jetzt sind wir uns alle einig." Geschrieben wird dieser eigenartige Mischmasch aus beiden Sprachen nicht gerade besser. Das fällt besonders auf, wenn mündliche Interviews in der Fachpresse abgedruckt werden.

Ich versuche in Meetings, die auf Deutsch gehalten werden, nur englische Ausdrücke zu verwenden, wenn sie kürzer oder treffender sind als ihr deutsches Äquivalent oder wenn es gar keine deutschen Übersetzungen gibt. Trotzdem lande ich meistens bei einem englischen Anteil von einem Viertel.

Um den ständigen Wechsel zwischen beiden Sprachen zu vermeiden, habe ich mich deswegen für den ungewöhnlichen Schritt entschieden, ein Buch für den deutschen Markt hauptsächlich auf Englisch zu schreiben – abgesehen von einigen abgeschlossenen deutschen Teilen wie hier.

So wird das Ganze, zumindest für diejenigen mit einigermaßen guten Englischkenntnissen, leichter zu verstehen sein, als wenn alle fünf Sekunden von Deutsch auf Englisch umgeswitcht werden müsste. Es hat den weiteren Vorteil, dass ich die etwas lockere Schreibart der englischen Sprache anwenden darf – und natürlich, dass das Ganze für mich einfacher wird zu schreiben. That's my excuse and I'm sticking to it.

Warum Fachbücher kurz und leicht zu lesen sein sollten

Vor Jahren hatte ich einen Kunden, bei dem die Länge der Meetings nur schwer einzuschätzen war. Ich habe deshalb drei Jahre lang relativ viel Zeit an einem der größten Hauptbahnhöfe Deutschlands verbracht. Zum Glück gab es dort eine Buchhandlung mit einer erstaunlich gut sortierten Fachbuchabteilung – offensichtlich war ich nicht der Einzige mit ferngesteuerten Reiseplänen. Ich habe dort oft Marketingbücher gekauft – meistens auf Englisch(!) – und gleich danach im Zug angefangen zu lesen.

Leider lässt bei mir nach langen Meetings und ungefähr einer halben Stunde Bahnfahrt oft die Konzentration nach. Die Mitreisenden oder die Landschaft werden plötzlich viel interessanter als das Geschriebene oder ich nicke einfach ein. Nur in den seltensten Fällen komme ich später dazu, das angefangene Buch weiter zu lesen. Als Konsequenz habe ich zu Hause ein ganzes Regal voll mit Büchern, in denen ein Lesezeichen des Bahnhofsbuchhändlers steckt, meistens in der Nähe von Seite 29. Aus vielen Gesprächen mit Kollegen habe ich erfahren, dass mein Verhalten nicht untypisch ist und die meisten Fachbücher ein ähnliches Schicksal erleiden.

Diese Erfahrungen und weitere Gespräche haben zu folgenden Insights über Bücher, insbesondere Fachbücher, geführt. Sie sind zwar nicht hundertprozentig empirisch bewiesen, werden aber in vielen Fällen trotzdem stimmen. Daraus habe ich auch Learnings abgeleitet:

- Die meisten Menschen in Deutschland besitzen viele Bücher, die sie noch nicht gelesen haben – viele davon waren Geschenke.

- Unter diesen ungelesenen Büchern sind einige, die mit großer Wahrscheinlichkeit **nie** gelesen werden – egal, wie lange sie im Regal Staub ansammeln.

- Je länger ein Buch ungelesen im Regal verweilt, desto unwahrscheinlicher ist es, dass es je gelesen wird.

- Bei Fachbüchern sieht es ähnlich aus, allerdings werden hier meistens die Inhaltsverzeichnisse und manchmal sogar die ersten Kapitel gelesen. Das hängt unter anderem mit dem hohen Kaufpreis zusammen, aber auch mit dem Bedürfnis mitreden zu können – zumindest mit allen anderen, die ebenfalls das Inhaltsverzeichnis und Kapitel 1 überflogen haben.

- Dieses Verhalten hat selten mit Faulheit oder schlechten Absichten zu tun, sondern vielmehr mit fehlender Zeit. Fachbücher sind meistens schwere Kost, die einen klaren Kopf und Konzentration erfordern. Leicht konsumierbare Alternativen wie Zeitschriften und Tagespresse werden daher oft vorgezogen.

- Fachbücher werden deshalb oft in den Urlaub mitgenommen, wo man hofft, mehr Zeit für die restlichen Kapitel zu finden. Viele Bücher treten dann zwar die Hin- und Rückreise an, landen aber unangetastet wieder im Regal.

Learnings

Vorausgesetzt, dass diese Insights allgemeine Gültigkeit besitzen, können daraus Konsequenzen gezogen werden, wenn man selbst dabei ist, etwas „Fachliches" zu verfassen. Ich habe drei Anhaltspunkte gefunden. Wer etwas schreibt, sollte:

1. **Sich kurz fassen.** Zeit ist das kostbarste Gut für die meisten Menschen, insbesondere für Manager.

2. **In leicht konsumierbaren Häppchen schreiben.** Es besteht viel öfter die Möglichkeit kurz reinzulesen als die Gelegenheit, langwierige Kapitel durch zu arbeiten.

3. **Einen Nutzwert mitliefern.** Auch eine kleine Zeitinvestition sollte sich womöglich auszahlen.

„Consumer Insights – Love them and leverage them" ist deswegen auf etwas über 120 Seiten begrenzt, leicht portioniert und wirkt hoffentlich sogar effektivitäts- und effizienzsteigernd bei zukünftigen Marketingaktivitäten.

Und wenn nicht, dürfte ein Lesezeichen bei Seite 29 die Uniformität im Bücherregal garantieren.

Consumer Insights – loving them

There are people who feel comfortable dealing with abstract ideas while others prefer more tangible tasks. Working with Consumer Insights starts off on a theoretical level but it's a means to a very concrete goal – more success – giving almost everyone involved with brands an incentive to like insights from the start. Before you can begin to love* them, though, you have to know a good deal more about insights and where and how they can be found.

This first and largest section attempts to deepen understanding of exactly what insights are, explain why they are so useful to brands and help make the search for them more productive. Ideally, having read it, you will begin to view insights as being like a puzzle that is begging to be solved.

Working with Consumer Insights can also be an emotional affair. The welcome sense of recognition that you feel when you first identify an insight with high potential is little different to the response that consumers have when that same thought is integrated into a brand's communication or the product itself.

If the insights bug does bite you, you may end up loving them purely for the success they bring, which is fine. But hopefully, like me, you will also find working with insights both fascinating and challenging.

*I was debating with myself whether to use the word "love" at all in this context as it is one of those words that has been debased by too frequent usage. Generations of visiting US rock bands, Oscar winners and people who have known each other for more than ten minutes have made declarations of love too much of an everyday occurrence. Then I realised that here too the word "love" is being used as a convenient abbreviation for getting really excited about something and liking it as a result which somehow makes it all right again No-one is being expected to fall head over heels for a Consumer Insight – even a beautiful one – just to appreciate what they can lead to.

Definitions of Consumer Insights – and why there's no need to agree on just one

Some people claim there are two categories of people: those who are always putting things into two categories and those who aren't. I often find such oversimplifications to be more useful than they perhaps deserve to be.

Imagine, for example, having to split candidates for a vacant job this way. The categories could include "leaders" versus "followers," "those who simplify things" versus "those who complicate things" and "problem-solvers" versus "problem-makers." Automatically, you could compile a short list of who is probably right to do a certain job and who almost certainly isn't.

Words and phrases in the business world can be split into two categories as well – those that have clear and precise meanings and those that don't.

We can be thankful that the "clear and precise" category exists. Expressions such as "depreciation" and "return-on-investment" must signal exactly the same thing to people regardless of where they work – if only so that they can then decide which of the five or more methods of each they want to apply.

Words and phrases in the "not so clear and precise" category are actually more like concepts, with the precise meaning depending as much on your opinion and experience than anything else. "Integrated communication," "equal opportunity" and "creative" are good examples of this second category – and yes, "Consumer Insights" can be found here too.

The lack of clarity for such vocabulary obviously tempts certain people to define such phrases for themselves. This helps explain the quite different definitions of Consumer Insights that can be found, which cover a surprisingly wide range of meaning. Interestingly, none of them can really be disagreed with.

Here are three, quite different definitions that I find particularly helpful:

Consumer Insights are:

- „Destilliertes Wissen und Erkenntnisse über das Verbraucherverhalten, über deren Bedürfnisse,

Gewohnheiten, Einstellungen, Motive und Erwartungen, die relevant für ein Produkt und eine Marke sind". (Marketing Lexikon, erweitert)

- "A penetrating, discerning understanding that unlocks an opportunity." (David Taylor, Added Value)
- "A revelation that makes your management, stockholders, brand team, innovation, R&D, designers, advertising agency and every person on earth go aha!" (Acupoll)

You can make a strong case for any of the above although personally I prefer the last two. This is simply because they not only describe what insights are but also imply that it's only when they are leveraged that they are truly useful.

This brings us, conveniently, to the heart of the issue.

The most interesting paradox in marketing

The concept of "Consumer Insights" is almost as old as marketing itself, which must mean it's approaching its 50th birthday. Most marketing professionals today have a fair understanding of what Consumer Insights are, even if they define them slightly differently – see above. Many, too, realise that insights are a powerful tool when applied properly, so it's rather surprising to realise just how few of the marketing activities these professionals develop actually leverage Consumer Insights. Something doesn't quite add up.

The average 20-spot prime time advertising block contains perhaps one insight-driven film – and remember that prime time tends to be booked by large companies with sizeable marketing departments who presumably are more professional than most. Products and packaging which reflect insights directly are just as rare and if you spot anything that remotely resembles an insight lurking behind the idea for an event, sponsoring deal or a website then you're either far more observant than I am or just plain generous.

So why the paradox? Why is it that something considered to be powerful by most marketers and which is available to everyone is used so rarely? Why is it that when a brand such as Dove bases their whole brand platform on Consumer Insights and the marketing world applauds their efforts as one, so few other companies end up following their lead?

I believe there are two main reasons for the dissonance between belief and behaviour here. Firstly, strong Consumer Insights are not as easy to find and mould into a manageable form as they first appear. Anyone who works with them regularly will know just how much time and effort is involved before the results are just right – and time is in short supply.

Secondly, even strong insights rarely "make it to market." Before they can find themselves reflected in marketing activities, they have to surmount a veritable obstacle course in the development process. An insight is often in competition with other criteria that "simply have to be" fulfilled by the activities being developed. And, as reflecting them is not the easiest criterion to fulfil when developing marketing activities, insights often simply drop off the radar, maintaining an existence only in documents and briefings – but not in any real-life activities to which consumers are exposed.

The most interesting paradox in marketing need not continue to exist. If enough marketing professionals understand that leveraging insights is a "must" rather than a "nice-to-do" then it will simply disappear. And, as a result, the world of marketing activities will be far more interesting for both consumers and marketers.

The case for leveraging Consumer Insights whenever possible

In order for this book to be helpful, the reader will have to buy into or at least understand and accept the thinking behind leveraging Consumer Insights wherever possible. Here, then, in brief is the case as well as I can put it.

Even if you don't need convincing and are actively leveraging insights already, it can still act as a brief reminder of why you are right to be doing so.

It starts with undifferentiated product performance

In almost all product and service categories nowadays, branded and unbranded products compete for the same customers. While most manufacturers can tell you how their product differs from and is possibly even better than the competition, what really counts is how consumers experience products.

From the consumers' perspective, most competing brands offer pretty much the same functional benefits. Very often, even if there are measurable differences in product performance they are not noticeable to the consumers who use them. With the exception of attributes that can easily be evaluated such as taste, smell and design consumers are simply not in a position to compare product performance – how many of them own an analytic laboratory?

As a result, consumers have little choice but to rely on the brand names themselves to "know" that a product will be good – definitely not the worst thing for marketers! Additionally, where appropriate and available, they can read independent tests, which relieve them of the evaluation task completely – "you will find this wine tastes wonderful".

The result of such "effective performance parity" in consumers' eyes is that pure product performance is rarely enough, by itself, to cause anyone to buy a particular branded product instead of the competition. The purchase decision depends on additional factors.

How most purchase decisions are made

Of the handful of possible criteria that is ever relevant for purchase decisions (including the aforementioned taste, smell and design), two in particular are important, whatever the category concerned. There is no real surprise in knowing what they are, either.

Most consumers decide on a particular branded product based on either a., the price, or b., how relevant the brand is to them. Usually, it's a combination of both.

a. **The price**. A price-based decision does not, of course, mean an automatic choice for the cheapest product available, even though it is often wrongly understood this way. Instead, what counts is that the price has to be seen to be fair – the real meaning of value for money – combined with the simple fact that the consumer has to be able to afford it.

While unimaginative retailers and worried manufacturers have been diligently training consumers to watch every last cent they spend, there are still many categories where the absolute price is not critical, only whether what is being purchased is believed to be worth it or not.

A great example here is the continued success of espresso pads that are a very expensive way of buying portioned ground beans and making coffee. Obviously, the convenience benefits that espresso pads offer consumers outweigh the premium they have to pay versus a normal packet of espresso.

b. **How relevant the brand is to the consumer**. Brands, as we all know by now, are not actually manufactured in factories but constructed in consumers' minds. Consumers know hundreds of brands, most of which they never buy – a fact which should make marketers who place too high a value on creating brand awareness think twice. Most brands are associated with a set of feelings and attitudes that go far beyond what the product actually does.

Just remind yourself that this is true. Think briefly of three large brands – Lego, Kaufhof and Apple – and compare what immediately comes to mind when considering each one. Which of the three brands immediately invokes associations that go much further than what the brand actually sells?

Of the many brands we all know, only those that fit

in with our needs and with our lives are considered for purchase. This obviously happens on a functional level, where we buy only things we (think we) can use. However, remembering we are dealing with "effective performance parity" here, it also has to happen on an emotional level in order for us to choose between brands. Fortunately, it is far easier to differentiate one brand from the next this way – it's what good branding is all about.

Compare your feelings again on three other brands, this time within the same category – United Airlines, Singapore Airlines and Qantas. All offer pretty much the same thing (ignoring differences in destinations) yet they evoke very different reactions, most of which have little to do with any actual experience of flying with the airline. Ask yourself which carrier you would prefer to fly to Hong Kong with? Then ask yourself if it would be the same airline for a business and a leisure trip?

One way to (over) simplify this argument is to say that when a particular branded product is bought it is because the product fits into our lives functionally while the brand fits emotionally.

The simple choice for manufacturers

Given the above, all manufacturers face a similar basic choice: either, a., compete essentially on price or b., become the most relevant brand for at least some of the consumers within the Target Group.

a. **Competing on price.** With very few exceptions, such as Ryanair and Lidl, competing only on price has more to do with tactical marketing than building long-term brand equity. It's risky, too. There's always someone who will offer a product or service cheaper than you do, even if only for a while until the next one decides to cut the price even further. What's more, the cost leadership that allows you to be the least expensive will erode over time as methods and practices are copied and become the standard. We tend to respect the handful of successful, high profile, low price companies and conveniently forget that most of them simply tick over in the marketing background or just run out of money.

b. **Become the most relevant for consumers**. This option has far more potential, as we will see.

Making a brand the most relevant for consumers

The best way of making a brand relevant for consumers is by demonstrating an understanding of them and the role that the product and its benefit play in their lives. Empathy has always been a salesman's best weapon and it is no different when the salesman is a brand.

Yet a salesman has an advantage over a brand when selling because he usually has sufficient time and exposure to sell in depth and answer questions. Brands have to build up their empathy with consumers quickly, via a series of short, one-way exposures.

The best way for a brand to demonstrate consumer understanding this way is by taking small, manageable nuggets of information about consumers – the Consumer Insights – and addressing them directly. Knowing what consumers want and need in their lives, a company can leverage such knowledge and let their brand be the "answer" to whatever is missing.

Once a brand has found and is leveraging strong Consumer Insights, it has an automatic empathy advantage over those competitors who are not doing so – everyone has a soft spot for someone who understands them and automatically likes those brands that appear to do so too.

With the exception of having an obviously better product, leveraging Consumer Insights is the surest and most effective way of achieving brand preference. And the principle can be used across all aspects of the marketing mix.

Leveraging insights for all marketing activities

The marketing activity associated closest with leveraging insights is, of course, communication. This is no surprise as the main reason to invest in advertising, aside from providing information, is to convince consumers to buy a particular product or service. TV Spots, advertisements, etc. offer the purest opportunity to present first the insight – "Oh look, they understand me" – and then the brand's answer to it – "Oh look, they understand me and they're addressing my needs".

Yet the same approach can be just as effective in other areas of marketing. For example:

- **Product development**, or improvement, is far more effective when the consumers' viewpoint is added to those of the R&D department and the finance director. The success rate for new product introductions can be increased dramatically when consumers are included in the development process from the start and not simply exposed to the results.

- **Packaging design** is more effective when consumers' concerns are added to those of the material and design experts. It may be a sobering thought for designers but consumers are far less concerned with the looks and aesthetics of most products as they are with the practical nature of the packages themselves – opening them, storing them and disposing of them. Even the appeal of the most beautiful design will not help resolve negative feelings towards a brand that has ignored these practical aspects of packaging.

- **Promotions, events, dialogue marketing, incentive programmes, etc.** can all benefit from an insight-driven approach once it is also understood what role such activities play in consumers' lives. Picking up yet another mail shot from the doormat, for example, is not the highlight of most people's days.

Why insights have never been more important

"There's nothing much new about Consumer Insights – people have been talking about them for decades. I remember working with P&G years ago and they were always going on about what consumers think, what they thought they were thinking and what they should be thinking. It's nothing we need to worry about, it's just become more fashionable, that's all."

If you were to own a collection of the best management and marketing books from the last 50 years, together with key articles that have appeared in the appropriate trade press, and somehow managed to find time to read all of them, you would soon realise something rather sobering. Almost all of the "hot" topics that concern us nowadays (with the exception of those created by new technologies) have been written about many times before.

Whether it's competitive advantage, customer orientation, quality management or cost leadership, etc. it is rare that anything genuinely new ever appears – it usually just resurfaces under another name. The continual rotation of marketing personnel ensures both that someone will "discover" most topics again and that they will appear to be fresh.

The idea of using Consumer Insights has certainly been around for many years and, in a way, acting directly upon insights is marketing in "Reinkultur." Allowing potential users to decide what should be made, not the manufacturer, is the whole idea behind marketing.

So why is being "consumer-centric," "being lead by consumers," "just listening" or, indeed, being insight-driven so relevant to companies nowadays? Why are so many companies suddenly rediscovering their "commitment to the consumer"? There appear to be two main reasons why the time has come for Consumer Insights – quality and speed.

Quality. The quality of goods has increased tremendously in recent years, at least in terms of them doing the job they are intended to do. For a whole variety of reasons, most of them good, tyres rarely go flat, a supermarket-bought yoghurt is almost never mouldy, cars hardly ever break down and even the cheapest washing machine will get your clothes clean.

Every DVD player you can buy from 29 to 1029 Euros plays DVDs well enough to watch them enjoyably. Compare this to the miserable performance of a cheap tape recorder only a few years ago.

For less discerning customers and the large number of consumers who watch their finances carefully, the "dangers" of buying cheaply nowadays are pretty small. So, with superior quality frequently hard to demonstrate and design often being a matter of taste (just look at the average furniture shop!), manufacturers have "only" their brand to fall back on.

Speed. Product lifecycles are becoming shorter and shorter; a fact that has more to do with technological advances than an increase in consumer impatience.

In categories with a steep innovation curve, manufacturers often find themselves having to develop marketing activities for products that they have not only never seen but which are still under development. Once on the market, it is already clear when they will be replaced, if not by what.

Even with more mundane innovations, the window of time that one manufacturer has to offer a unique or a superior product before the competition offers something of similar quality – or simply copies it – has never been so short.

With product performance and features, even design, easier than ever to match, it is only a brand itself that can remain unique over time.

Given this combination of high quality products and fast imitation, it is likely that the consumer will be the focus of attention for most companies for many years to come.

⊙ How about...

... some of the categories, which are characterised by selling product features or pushing only price, suddenly discovering Consumer Insights?

Take the computer market, for example. Currently, the extent to which insights are taken into account by most PC manufacturers is to describe certain machines as being suitable "for beginners", "gamers (!)" or the "advanced user," whatever that means. Yet consumers' computer needs surely extend to other dimensions as well.

What if more manufacturers, for example, were to focus

on how quiet their machines are, make them look completely different or even capitalise on the fact that many people attribute their computer with almost human qualities – "she's in a bad mood today". Maybe they wouldn't have to talk so much about specifications that few potential buyers understand – or the low prices that they clearly do.

Why there are suddenly so many Insights Departments

" I was reading recently that yet another of the multinationals has installed an Insights Department to underline their "commitment to the consumer". What I was wondering was where did all of these specialists suddenly come from. Are they really experts – and what were they doing up until now?"

In their desire to focus more on consumers and be less manufacturer-orientated, a number of companies have installed Consumer Insights functions in recent years, although the name of the department sometimes differs. You would not have found a "Global Insight Manager" or a 20-man "Insights Team" anywhere ten years ago but neither is a rarity nowadays.

Interestingly, this development has taken place at the very same time as most companies have been shedding staff rather than taking on new ones, which does make you wonder how it was possible for completely new departments to be created without hardly anyone being hired.

The answer, usually, is that the new Consumer Insights department is the old Market Research department, which has been re-named to demonstrate the company's "renewed commitment" to taking their consumers seriously. Despite often having new leadership (one of the few people that has been hired) these departments usually continue doing pretty much the same thing they have been doing in the past, albeit with the possibility of being taken more seriously by Management than before.

Of course, whether re-naming a department is enough to make those who work there any more attuned to consumers' needs and feelings than they were before is questionable. The skill set and understanding of people that is necessary to spot strong insights and help turn them into marketing activities is almost certainly not the same one that qualified the market researchers for their jobs in the first place – usually an affinity for statistics and logical analysis.

The increase in Insights Departments is to be welcomed, if only to document how companies should be thinking nowadays. But, if it is only the name that ends up changing and the staff are not re-trained, we cannot really expect too much to change in the output from these companies either.

⊙ How about...

... more companies taking their stated "commitment to consumers" one step further than they do now? Instead of just parking the responsibility for marketing and brands with one of the other top functions, how about insisting that every company selling branded goods always automatically includes a Chief Marketing Officer or Chief Branding Officer in the "Vorstand" or "Geschäftsführung," just as there is always a CEO and a CFO?

This is not happening, currently. Paradoxically, at the same time that many companies are claiming an increased consumer orientation, the number of marketing staff at the very top level has actually decreased. This state of affairs is particularly unfortunate in a growing economy; whilst cost controllers should ensure that a company remains profitable, the number of brands that have been built by finance directors can be counted on the fingers of one hand.

Strangely, in Germany, the bigger a company is, the less likely you are to find a trained brand/marketing person amongst the top echelons. Banks, other financial institutions, pharmaceutical and chemical companies are among the major culprits here, but they are not alone.

This goes some way to explain why the country that exports more goods and services than any other in the world actually owns far fewer international brands than a country of its size should.

Why the term "Consumer Insights" is not always referring to the same idea

"I have a lot of dealings with Direct Mail companies or as they prefer to be called, Dialogue Marketers. I must say, their methods and tools have become very sophisticated and the depth of the data they can deliver is quite astounding. I've noticed, though, that more and more of these companies claim that what they are dealing with are Consumer Insights."

Dialogue Marketing companies can obtain far more detailed data about markets, consumers and potential consumers than ever before. It is now possible to analyse this data, make smart analyses and produce far shorter mailing lists. This significantly increases the likelihood that the person receiving a mail shot is actually interested in what it is being sold.

In fact, one of the reasons for the steady increase in Dialogue Marketing expenditure in recent years is not an increased acceptance by the recipients of such material (does anyone really **want** to receive what they are sent? Do you?), but an increase in the cost effectiveness of such activities. Due to far better targeting, "Streuverlust", a frequently misunderstood concept, has been reduced considerably and the efficiency of dialogue marketing increased as a result.

(It is not always easy to make this case. My children receive mail shots every month from companies offering them easy credit or inexpensive holidays, while my name seems to appear on the mailing list of every English language school in Hamburg.)

Despite using the same terminology, when Dialogue Marketers talk about Consumer Insights they are not referring to what is being discussed at length here. There is a huge difference, for example, between knowing that the people most likely to buy a certain convertible live in certain parts of large cities, have a minimum of two credit cards and frequently buy products on-line (part of a Dialogue Marketer's version of a Consumer Insight) and knowing what owning and driving a particular cabriolet means to these people.

Another way of looking at it would be that while Dialogue Marketing's Consumer Insights are concerned mostly with **what** is happening (valuable information), the phrase is also used here to understand **how** and **why** things are happening – information that is even more valuable.

Other companies claiming to be selling insights include purveyors of quantitative surveys and the management consultants who analyse the data – again, very interesting, but not the same product.

It's unfortunate, in a way, that the same term is used to describe related but dissimilar kinds of information; however, once the differences are clear, most companies realise that they probably could use a little bit of all of them at one time or another.

Why successful products leverage insights whether it was planned that way or not

"I'm fed up with reading about companies being consumer-centric, having a consumer orientation etc. Lots of different approaches to marketing work, not just that one. Look at most of the successful products on the market – they didn't look for Consumer Insights first, they just got on with it. They were either better products than their competitors or they had great advertising or both."

There are many roads to success (though not quite as many as there are to failure) and taking the "leveraging insights" approach isn't a pre-requisite for creating a winning product. This doesn't mean, however, that just because insights weren't being used actively to create products that they weren't behind their success nonetheless.

It could be argued that if a branded product has been successful, then it must have been relevant to consumers which, in turn, means it must have been addressing an insight, either consciously or otherwise. If not, no one would have bought it! But is this just a smart-arse argument or is there more behind it?

Companies are always frustrated when their meticulously developed products and services leave consumers shrugging their shoulders. Every year, articles are published informing us that only a quarter or even less of the new products introduced the previous year were successful.

Is this failure rate simply the result of manufacturers choosing to ignore insights? Of course it isn't but take a close look at the main reasons that experts claim are responsible for failure.

According to most experts, new product introductions that fail are:

- Nothing new, me-too's, just a version of something already known
- Too expensive or bad value
- Insufficiently supported with marketing investment
- Badly timed – too early, too late, at the wrong time of year
- Badly designed, etc.

Oh, there is one more:

- Not relevant to consumer needs.

Looking at this list, something soon becomes quite apparent. Most of the reasons seen for the failure of new product introductions are under the direct control of the companies who launched them. If they could be more honest with themselves, they would know when they are just copying another company's success, know if they are investing too little in marketing support and know if they are offering bad value for money. In other words, companies can decide for themselves whether to risk failing for one of these reasons.

The one reason for failure that companies don't automatically have under their control is the one about consumer relevance – knowing whether their new product really does answer a consumer need or desire. Yet this knowledge is there for the taking if a company only takes the trouble to do so.

How many of the product failures from last year or any other year could have been avoided if the manufacturers had listened more to what consumers were prepared to tell them if only they had been consulted? Why would a company not attempt to reduce the high risks involved with launching new products by doing so?

◉ How about...

... every single request for a product development project in a company being accompanied not only by a list of desired product attributes but also by a clear, written statement of the insight(s) that the new product or packaging should be addressing?

Implementing such a system would automatically decrease the number of projects in development, as evidence of their potential would not be available. This is likely to make most R&D departments very happy. A further advantage would be that the marketing process would begin far earlier in the product development cycle than is usually the case, representing even more progress.

Projected over time, the marketplace would be home to even more insight-driven offerings than it is now. Who knows, it might even lead to dust-resistant laptop screens and yoghurts that don't stick to the lid!

Why listening to consumers makes more sense than many interested parties give credit for

"I'm of the opinion that asking consumers about everything you're planning to do is overrated – it's just trying to get someone else to do your job for you, isn't it? Consumers can't be expected to evaluate things that don't exist yet, they can only tell you about what they already know. Just look what happens if you ask consumers what advertising should look like: they repeat the same tired clichés that they themselves don't like any more. So why are we so keen on hearing what they have to say about everything else? I'd much rather trust my own intuition."

Even if we might be happy for them to do so, consumers can't do our work for us. By definition, consumers are "just" normal people and they're not suddenly going to give us the idea for the next Red Bull-style success in the middle of an interview above a bakery or sketch out a storyboard on their complimentary notepads during a group discussion.

Yet questioning the value of listening to consumers when developing products and marketing activities is rather short-sighted. The argument usually made is that consumers could never have imagined products such as the Walkman, the iPod, Google, etc. and that real innovation can only come from genius at work. It is further pointed out that consumers usually reject wildly new creative ideas simply because they are so different.

While some of this thinking is valid, the conclusion that you can't get ideas for the future from consumers simply indicates that those making the argument don't know how to ask.

Take, for example, the original Walkman. We all know that it wasn't a wildly inventive consumer who suddenly jumped up and shouted: "Hey! I would love a portable tape recorder that I can listen to on headphones while I'm out and about and is tough enough to be taken jogging – and I don't care if it does eat a set of batteries a day." Yet, if asked the right questions, potential Walkman consumers would readily have confided that they would like to isolate themselves from their surroundings sometimes and that they would appreciate listening to their own music while not at home. The Walkman could easily have been the result of listening to such unmet consumer needs – and the smart people at Sony were certainly well tuned in to what consumers were missing in their lives.

Similarly, consumers who had discovered the joy of free music were crying out for MP3 software that was simple enough for a child to use (a phrase that hardly applies any more to technical gadgets) even if they didn't add "and make it in a really hip design". And early Internet users were often frustrated by the huge amount of unfiltered information suddenly available at their fingertips and latently looking for a way to bring order to their information needs.

One way of looking at things is that talking to consumers helps determine what questions need to be answered. The answers themselves still have to come from companies – but if they don't know the questions, how will they ever come up with any?

◉ How about...

... those being paid to be creative seeing consumers as more than just a hurdle to be negotiated before an idea is allowed to flourish? Rather than being frustrated that the general public doesn't see things the way one would like them to, why not learn to create ideas that match the way that most consumers really think? How about embracing the mainstream?

There is a tendency amongst marketers and agencies to look down on anything that is mainstream, yet out and out success can be found only if a brand can tap into it. And who better to tell you about what the mainstream likes than those who make up its numbers?

Relying on intuition works for about 5% of marketers and they are to be envied. The rest of us should be thankful that consumers are so talkative.

Why you have to understand the barriers to purchase for a brand or product

"My chief editor doesn't understand the ways of the world any more. He spent months with his team reworking every aspect of the magazine – the layout, the style of writing – all of it. We even commission most of the photography ourselves. By any objective measure, our magazine is now better than our main competitor and it even costs a little less on the shelf. Yet, since the relaunch, we haven't seen any movement in the circulation at all – he's so frustrated."

As most marketing plans ask for growth, most marketing activities are designed to attract new users to a brand. The usual way to go about this is to communicate to potential consumers what the advantages of a brand are and wait for them to run to the shops. Unfortunately, even when a brand makes a good case and communicates it effectively to its Target Group few, if any, of the potential new users actually take the bait. Why is that?

Consumers aren't just sitting around waiting to be enticed to purchase every product offered. And the competition isn't usually just sitting around waiting for others to poach their customers. Fortunately for all brand owners, there is a high level of inertia in the system, which prevents market shares yo-yo-ing from one period to the next.

Often, though, there are also concrete reasons why certain consumers have decided actively not to buy a particular product or brand. And as long as these barriers to purchase are not addressed, a sale will never be made.

One manufacturer of men's cologne, for example, found out that his product signalled to others that the man wearing it was completely under the thumb of his wife – and the product had a very distinctive fragrance!

Ask yourself just how superior the products from some car-makers would have to be in terms of design, technology or any other parameter important to you before you would consider sitting behind the wheel and driving to a business meeting in one? The apparent stigma of rolling up in the car park in a vehicle with the "wrong" emblem on the bonnet is hard to counter.

Let's look a little closer at an example that we can probably all relate to – the acceptable face of gambling that is the state-run 6 out of 49 Lotto. For years, the marketing departments of the various regional Lotto organisations have been trying to win over new players to the game. Yet, for the most part, it's the same, admittedly large group of people who fill out their tickets every week and hope anew that their life will be changed by Saturday evening.

Over the years, this particular form of inertia has meant that the only sure way for the Lotto organisations to increase their revenue has been to make an unpopular price increase and hope for low price elasticity – " I always fill out exactly eight boxes." Nowadays, with consumers not only having less to spend but also with many more gambling options available, organic growth seems even less likely.

But what are the main reasons why people who don't play Lotto don't play?

- They don't gamble on anything
- They can't afford to/don't want to spend the money
- They consider the 140 million-to-1 odds of winning the jackpot to be just a little unfavourable
- They can't identify with the game and don't want to be seen as Lotto players.

Of these four arguments, it's very hard to counter the first three. It's an uphill struggle to convince anyone to start doing something they are completely opposed to, people can't spend money they don't have, and Lotto does offer fairly lousy odds compared to other bets, even if the absolute size of the jackpot can be very tempting.

The last reason on the list, however, is one barrier to purchase that could be addressed over time as it has more to do with the image of the game and those who play it than the product itself. If the Lotto organisations were to make a concerted effort to change the image of the typical Lotto player then this barrier would start to erode.

For some reason, however, almost all of the "Lottogesellschaften" seem hell-bent on doing their best to perpetuate the negative image of the Lotto player, rather than change it! How do most Lotto organisations draw attention to their product? They show "ordinary" people suddenly transported to a life of luxury – and to accentuate how luck can favour absolutely anyone, they exaggerate just how "ordinary" these people really are. They're depicted as dim-witted, ignorant and crude ... and now rich as well. This is just what the non-Lotto-players always suspected.

As the Lotto organisations really do need to attract new users, the best thing for them to do now would be a 180-degree turn and start changing the image of the Lotto player. Even just showing that Lotto players are people like you and me (and not permanent residents of Ballerman 6) would be a good first step towards lowering this barrier to purchase, rather than bolstering it.

The resulting communication might end up being less entertaining – but it might just end up working, too.

⊙ How about...

... trying to find out those things about your brand or product that potential consumers really don't like and which may even be actively preventing sales? Looking for negatives requires extreme honesty from manufacturers as it means facing the gap between their own "knowledge" of the brand and the "truth" as consumers see it. It's worth the effort, however, as the results can be very enlightening

Information about barriers to purchase won't always be immediately offered up in research, as consumers tend to be fairly polite in such situations. But if you are persistent and creative in getting to the heart of the issues, the problem areas will become clear. Often, the best way to discover your product's perceived failings is to find out just what it is about your competition that makes them so liked – most people would rather be complimentary than critical.

Some of the barriers found out this way will be a fixed part of your product and effectively unchangeable. Others, though, will be under your control and capable of being addressed if you are really serious about attracting new users. Just make sure you don't lose the current users in the process.

Why marketing teams should expand their horizons

"One thing that I find difficult when developing ideas and concepts is that they are often intended for people that aren't really that much like me. Of course, we check things with the others in the office, especially the juniors and the assistants, but often we're surprised when what we thought was a good idea bombs completely in research."

It's ironic that the very people in a company who are supposed to be closest to "normal" consumers often lead rather isolated lives. It's not that they are recluses or hermits – quite the opposite – but they do tend to move in certain, quite narrow circles and see little of what the "mass market" is really like. Usually, though, it's the mass market that they're dealing with.

Let's be a little clichéd and consider what the average marketer with a degree of responsibility for a brand is like: he (or she) drives a car to work, so doesn't use public transport, eats in (often expensive) restaurants or the company canteen, rather than eating a sandwich for lunch, reads a quality newspaper rather than a tabloid and accompanies his (or her) children, if he (or she) has any, to hockey practice where like-minded parents are gathered. (No pre-conceived notions here, of course.)

There's nothing at all wrong with living a life like this – but if you want to know what "the masses" are thinking, it's not very revealing. Interestingly, one of the less acknowledged reasons for friction between marketing and sales departments is that the latter can always tell when marketing people have lost touch a little with reality, with what's "normal." Sales teams get about more than most people and visit many places, some of which they might usually avoid – but they know the ground rules when they're there. Ideas from the more isolated of the marketing team, which obviously miss the mark, can be a huge source of irritation and extra work.

If this somewhat exaggerated scenario sounds at all familiar, here are three suggestions for those who feel they could use an extra injection of the normal:

- Ask your local supermarket if you can spend an afternoon working on the checkout. Observe what people buy, what combinations of product are placed on the conveyor belt and what sizes are bought. Watch how the mood of buyers seems to be when they are shopping and how much they are distracted, even embarrassed if they have children with them.

- Arrange to visit some consumers at home to watch your product being used. (Obviously, this won't work for everything.) Try to make yourself invisible and just observe what happens. Watch for how packages are opened, how products are used and where they are kept. Then ask some basic questions and be prepared for some unexpected answers.

- Go to work and back on public transport for a week, if you don't already do so. If this is not convenient, do it anyway – it's not always that convenient for those who rely on it. Take a newspaper, pretend to read it and, forgetting what you were taught about eavesdropping, listen to what other people are talking about. It's unlikely to be directly relevant to your brands but it will attune you more to how "normal" people think.

If you follow any of these suggestions then I guarantee that the next time new proposals for marketing activities are on the table, at least some of those general impressions you will have picked up will lead you to decide differently than had you not gone out for a dose of normality.

⊙ How about...

... marketing teams putting their pre-conceived notions about their products to one side for an afternoon and going insight gathering? This could be done simply by taking a fresh approach to store checks, talking to some consumers or by arranging some home visits – see above.

Everyone involved should act as if they were completely new to the category, writing down every relevant, potential insight that they encounter – even the seemingly banal. Then all notes should be combined.

The result should be a long list of possible insights, many of them known but some of which will not have appeared before or at least not expressed in that particular way. Some of these new or newly formulated observations may well be capable of being addressed in the brand's activities.

The list will also be interesting for what it doesn't contain. In most categories there are a number of givens – "facts" which are agreed by all involved to be right. If these givens don't appear on the list, then it might be time to re-assess what you believe to be true about your category – maybe the "facts" don't have such broad application after all.

Some teams may end up thinking afresh, for example, about why the largest detergent pack is sometimes bought by one-person households, why consumers compare the price of powdered espresso in cents on the shelves yet pay over the top for the cup of latte they drink in the coffee shop, or even why some pasta shapes are preferred when packed in bags rather than boxes.

Why you shouldn't be afraid of the seemingly obvious

"We spend a lot time looking for clever Consumer Insights for our biggest brand but not much new ever seems to come out of it. We always find out the same things we already know – people's needs don't seem to change much over time. That made it particularly annoying when our main competitor started addressing a fairly basic, almost banal insight in their communication – and it worked!"

There is a school of thought that claims that new, profound insights can only be discovered when psychologists with at least two Dr titles delve deeply into the psyche of a few unfortunates who are grilled for hours in a shadowy room until they reveal "the truth".

Certainly such techniques can be very revealing but you have to wonder whether anything buried that deep is really going to be applicable to the chosen Target Group as a whole. And, if it is applicable but was that well hidden, will they be prepared to admit it?

Most brands that have achieved significant success by leveraging Consumer Insights have not strayed too far from the generic attributes and benefits that their product category offers. Instead, they have focussed on Simple Truths, often quite basic observations about a brand or category which are actually quite obvious – but only once they have been pointed out to you. By building on such Simple Truths and linking their brand's benefits to the resulting insights, these companies have found new ways of making their brands more relevant.

This is exactly what the building society did that countered feelings amongst young rejecters of their product that financing property this way was old-fashioned and boring. They simply built on the Simple Truth that paying rent your whole life was not too smart either and showed that their product could help avoid doing so.

An even more obvious insight was leveraged by the importer of inexpensive cars to the U.K. who compared the comfort of having four doors on their model with the disadvantages of having only two doors on any other new car you could buy at that price.

Both of the above brands achieved their goals by forming insights out of Simple Truths and communicating basic product characteristics that now had new relevance for consumers.

This doesn't mean, of course, that anything that is blindingly obvious has insight potential. It still requires a smart, different answer to a basic desire, an outsider's view of the banal or even a child-like, see-something-for-the-first-time approach to turn a Simple Truth into something valuable.

⊙ How about...

... trying to identify the Simple Truths about the categories your brands are part of that would resonate with most consumers? Re-examine the basic benefits your product offers to see whether approaching them from a new angle will produce new ideas. It's not only the advantages of a product that can be re-assessed, almost all attributes, good or seemingly less good, have the potential to lead to something interesting.

What would happen, for example, if those responsible at the Post Office for encouraging people to write more letters, in order to sell more stamps, were to take this approach? Written letters appear to have few advantages over other forms of communication: e-mail and SMSs are faster, less formal and fashionable, while a phone call is two-way and instant. What is it about the old-fashioned method of sending letters by snail mail that could be leveraged versus modern competition?

Possibly the best Simple Truth to leverage would be the supposed disadvantage that writing a letter takes far more effort than any other form of communication. Surely this must signal to the recipient of a personal letter (and who gets many of these nowadays) that they must mean a lot to the person who has written it – otherwise the effort would not have been made.

A communication idea based on this insight, such as "If they're special, make sure it's a real letter" or, seen from the recipient's perspective, "If it's a letter, I must be special" would make this seemingly obvious attribute more relevant – and would certainly have more potential than simply enjoining people to write letters again.

Why store checks are so good for spotting insights

"I hate doing store checks and to be honest I've never really seen the point of them. You have to visit a huge number of shops before you can produce any reliable numbers and lots of shops don't like you standing there and writing things down – some even throw you out. I know what my products look like on a shelf and I've seen the competitor's too – so why should I bother?"

Most members of a marketing department consider conducting store checks to be an unimportant, lowly task. When they are seen to be necessary, it's usually the junior staff who are lumbered with the job and, more often than not, their reports are paid little attention to. Yet both this attitude towards store checks and the behaviour here are a huge mistake.

Some of the keenest store-checkers I have ever met have gone on to become MDs and CEOs and have then continued to check stores regularly after that as well. They always return to their offices with some action points or even new ideas. Apparently they know something that others don't.

Store checks can be an excellent tool but should not really be used to produce numbers. After all, most companies are paying large monthly fees to organisations that can provide far more reliable data. Instead, store checks should be conducted to provide fresh input about one's own and other, related categories, to watch and listen to consumers while they are shopping and, of course, to produce material for insights.

Rather than try to explain how to spot an insight when store checking (look, there's one, hiding behind the red cabbage) here are some pieces of information, which went on to be included in insight-driven concepts that were discovered simply by spending an afternoon wandering around the shops.

Products that include their proposed usage in the brand name, such as "Peaceful Night Tea" or "Working Mother Vitamins" are bought far more often on impulse than those that don't.

- Most people who take the top off personal care products to smell the fragrance wrinkle their nose and put it back on the shelf.

- Hardly anyone takes the time any more when buying eggs to see whether they are all intact. The sell-by dates are rarely looked at, either.

- If men aren't buying the cheapest beer, and most don't, they ignore minor price differences and take the brand they came in to buy, regardless of price.

- Women who visit the cosmetic departments of those hypermarkets that don't allow manufacturers to use their own shelf material stand around looking totally bemused by the sheer volume of what's on the shelves. If they can't find their own brand quickly, they usually buy what's on special display or nothing at all.

It is not difficult to work out what product, packaging and distribution innovations could follow from these insights – and they were there, waiting to be discovered by anyone who walked into the shops with an open mind.

◉ How about...

... conducting store checks religiously, once a month, no matter what else seems to have more priority? You don't have to go to the trouble of visiting different towns (although you should, if you get the chance), but you should visit stores in different areas that are within reach. While you're there, you could even do some shopping!

Why numbers can be the best source of qualitative insights

"It's all about how consumers think and feel, isn't it? Applied psychology, you might call it. That's why I never bother looking too much at statistics or other numbers – they're just cold facts that tell you nothing much about why people do stuff and that's what we need to know."

Earlier, the oversimplification of dividing people into two categories was discussed and here is another opportunity to do so by splitting up all marketers. "Those that feel good with numbers" and "those that are less comfortable with numbers" tend to be two categories of people who differ greatly in many of their attitudes.

The more extreme members of the smaller group, the "number lovers", often have an aversion to what cannot be quantified. This is why they are always trying to measure things, even those that don't lend themselves to calibration, such as creativity. At the other extreme, "number haters", often go so far as to refuse to see what numbers are telling them, even when it's very clear.

Interestingly, numbers can sometimes be the best way of finding out certain consumer characteristics because, as the old saying goes, you should judge people on what they do, not on what they say.

Consumers say many things that are not really true, especially in a research environment such as focus groups where their opinions are on public display. This is one of the main reasons why insights harvested this way need to be validated for broad application before they are actually used. People's actions, on the other hand, are as close to actual facts as you will get in marketing and these are often recorded in figures.

Reliable numbers on what consumers really do can be a good source of insights; sales figures, in-home diaries, product-in-use and Usage and Attitude data, etc. all provide information on what has happened with products rather than what was intended or maybe just said. Used properly, such information can lead to insights where qualitative studies would come up blank.

One example of numbers leading to insights that I was involved in concerned a popular convenience food brand. The out-of-stock figures were normal all week but dangerously high on Saturdays and far higher than any competitor. The product was not perishable so the stores themselves were not at fault by making sure they had none left over to rot at the weekend, meaning another factor had to be found.

Deeper analysis showed that the brand was bought mostly on Friday evenings and Saturdays, by consumers who left their weekend plans until the last moment. By building this knowledge into their delivery logistics, the company was able to increase sales significantly, while reducing the number of disappointed consumers at the same time. Additionally, the brand's communication was changed to reflect the mentality of these heavy users who up until then had been perceived by the company very differently.

⊙ How about...

... re-examining all of your important quantitative market research reports purely for the purpose of scanning them for insights?

By ignoring the original purpose of the documents and regardless of whether they are product tests or share reports, the results can be sifted through for interesting pointers to consumer behaviour.

Perhaps your product is used far more often in the morning than your competitors who are used more after work. Maybe yours is one of those rare brands with an appeal to younger and older women but not to those in between. Such phenomena are often put down to "technical glitches" but usually there are real explanations to be found. And if there are, you probably want to find out what they are and do something about it.

Why products must appeal to the heart and the head

"My Target Group is made up mostly of men who don't have much time to waste. They need to be talked to directly, given the facts and nothing else – they come to the right decisions by themselves. We don't need to dress up our message in niceties or humour – our product just sells itself. Not quite as much as it used to sell, though..."

Even the most rational people allow themselves to be guided by their emotions when shopping – although to what degree this happens depends on what they are buying. The strait-laced purchasing clerk who squeezes every cent from his suppliers at work may, without question, pay the asking price for an addition to his vintage comic collection. (He may even wear Sylvester the Cat underwear beneath his mouse-grey suit.)

"Normal" consumers make almost all of their purchase decisions on the basis of both rational reasoning and emotional desires. Knowing this, a brand has to provide an answer to both sides of the coin; it's not enough to give just the plain facts, especially when the products in a category differ only slightly and any brand could provide similar data. Yet neither is it sufficient to wrap up a generic message in emotional cotton wool and then brand it.

More often than we realise, consumers use rational arguments for a product as an alibi for a purchase that is a mostly emotional affair. The facts help to justify spending the money either to themselves or just as often to help explain to others why something "just must" be bought. Smart marketers understand this mechanism and feed in the necessary information.

For this reason, advertising for sports cars often talks about safety features at high speed, even though the makers know their cars are being bought for their looks and stunning 0-100 mph acceleration. Similarly, it's why the producers of certain expensive cosmetic brands spend time talking about their hypoallergenic nature (a pure marketing invention, by the way) knowing exactly why their highly priced products are really being bought – the more expensive the jar, the more hope will fit in it.

Even where hard, rational selling is believed to be the best way to convince the Target Group to buy a certain product, non-rational elements are still at work, usually addressing insights about the Target Group as a whole, rather than the category itself.

Take, for example, one of the most successful introductions of a cleaning product in recent years. In the TV advertising, the product is "hard-sold" directly to camera by a woman in a loud, confident, almost aggressive manner. What is different to previous attempts to shout the cleaning products consumer into submission is the character of the woman portrayed. Yes, she is loud and aggressive but she is also smart and charismatic and is obviously in charge. In fact, the woman portrayed is pretty much how many members of the Target Group would like to be themselves.

While the actual message of the TV spot is benefit driven and insight free, the execution leverages this knowledge about how the Target Group would like to be to make the message more acceptable. If the same film had been made with a man, it would probably have failed miserably.

◉ How about...

... the producers of more brands starting to think in terms of leveraging both rational and non-rational reasons for purchase, even in those categories where traditionally only one or the other has been used?

One of the most useful exercises in marketing is to find a good answer to the simple question "why should consumers buy my particular brand?" and then act accordingly. If both a rational and an emotional/psychological answer can be found and used then success is all that more likely.

If fashion brands did this, for example, they might start finding reasons for why their brand is the right one beyond the usual answer that it shows your sense of style and need to belong. Some fashion brands, shoes in particular, already do this, but why not try adding further rational factors such as quality of finish, responsible sourcing or even skin-feel to the mix? Most fashion advertising to be found in women's magazine is completely interchangeable in terms of what is being said, so such an approach could only improve things.

At the other end of the spectrum, manufacturers of computer hardware might venture beyond simply listing product specifications (most of which the Target Group doesn't understand anyway) and frame them in consumer terms. Here, a first step might be to talk about time saving rather than speed, or about foolproof installation rather than compatibility.

In almost any category a company could try to provide both rational and emotional reasons to want their brand. Even extreme cases such as hypermarkets, if they really wanted to, could find a reason why customers should visit their particular shop that isn't based on pricing or parking. They may even end up making some money at last, too.

Why the more a product is seen to be a luxury, the trickier it is to leverage insights

"Our company sells its image and heritage as much as its products. Everything we make is of the finest quality and very often it would be impossible to make our products better no matter how hard you tried. But without our logo on them, they wouldn't find many buyers. Our prices are high, of course, but this is an advantage – it helps demonstrate the luxury nature of the brand and ensures that only certain people can afford it."

What products immediately come to mind when we hear the word "luxury?" Fur coats, expensive jewellery, handbags, five-star hotels etc. Luxury, of course, doesn't have to be expensive in absolute terms, just relative ones: handmade chocolates that cost two euros each are a luxury as well, although almost everyone could afford them if they wanted to.

A somewhat cynical but nonetheless accurate definition of what constitutes luxury goods is that they aren't really necessary at all. They do not fulfil basic consumer needs; neither do they solve any problems that consumers might have. Instead, they play a more complex, hedonistic role in people's lives – consumers just want to own them – which is why the insight approach is rather limited for most luxuries.

Leveraging insights tends to work best when specific issues can be identified and addressed. This kind of problem/solution approach, even if well disguised, is where the leverage can be the most effective as the difference between "before" and "after" is most noticeable. Where there is no specific issue to be addressed, just a strong desire to own, say, a particular brand of shoes or high-end loudspeakers, then there is far less to leverage.

There are, however, ways of applying general insights to luxury products, especially where barriers to purchase are concerned. Many consumers face conflicting emotions when considering buying luxuries and have, somehow, to justify to themselves and others that the purchase is not simply indulgence. Certain luxury brands manage to help consumers resolve these inner conflicts.

One brand of high-end loudspeakers, for example, is justified with the unbelievable difference to the listening experience that they can make for everybody. Technical specifications are used, for example, to show how low distortion levels are at peak volume although, in reality, the system will rarely be turned up loud enough for the neighbours even to consider complaining.

Another, more emotional approach taken by one watch company helps potential buyers justify paying thousands of euros more than necessary to have the time on their wrist by informing them that the purchase is not an indulgence at all but an investment that will be handed on to the next generation.

By understanding the nature of the barriers to purchase for luxury goods and finding the appropriate answer for the category concerned, even the manufacturers of such premium products can use insights to help differentiate their brand from the many other, high-priced competitors.

◉ How about...

... more manufacturers of luxury goods trying to leverage insights, even if the products, traditionally, have relied on image and values? One possibility, as we have seen, is to address the barriers to purchase but perhaps there are others to be found too.

Could custom-made shoes be sold, for example, by arguing that feet suffer in silence when footwear doesn't fit perfectly? Perhaps luxury chocolates (two euros each, remember) could be sold with the idea that having decided to eat less sweet things, you should eat only the best when you do indulge yourself.

While a great image may always be the most important success factor for these "nice to have" products, the insight approach should at least be attempted by the many luxury brands who occupy the second tier.

Why you shouldn't fall in love with an insight without validating it first

"When I heard that focus group talking about their young children and the difficulties of finding something every day that the whole family would eat I felt like I could have been sitting there myself saying exactly the same thing. That's why I was so confident that the concept itself would work – and so disappointed when it didn't. Maybe we should have checked the idea properly beforehand but it just seemed so right..."

We are all guilty, sometimes, of believing that most people think pretty much like we do ourselves, even though the evidence points to everyone being rather different. So when an idea appeals to us personally, without the need for any long explanation we're tempted to assume that everyone else will react that way to it too and see little need to confirm our feelings.

It is rare, however, that those making the marketing decisions are part of the Target Group. And, even when they are, they still represent only one opinion: an informed, intelligent, articulate opinion probably, but still just one. It is something of a conceit and frequently an expensive mistake to believe that you can know what a group of people will think about something without asking at least some of them first. Even if experience of products and categories does build up a fair sense of what will work, no-one's judgment is infallible.

I have often heard colleagues giggling when, say, the product manager for a tampon brand is male, the marketing director for a leading cigarette doesn't smoke or the agency's account director for a shampoo brand has no hair. While such pairings are probably not ideal, at least they mean that the people involved tend not to get sidetracked by their own opinions as much as if they believed they knew everything there is to know about a category.

Validating an insight is not difficult. Sometimes, it is enough to check it against existing data and previous experience or simply ask the other experts in the company. If there is still any uncertainty, however, the smart thing to do is ask the Target Group itself.

Small scale, insight-driven concept checking need be neither expensive nor particularly time consuming as the research has a very specific goal – to determine how broadly the chosen concepts can be applied to the Target Group. Often it is enough to use just verbal descriptions, which makes lead-in times short, and sample sizes can be modest, just big enough to determine some basic numbers. Results can be available within days of deciding that some confirmation of intuition is needed.

The results may sometimes be disappointing – but nowhere near as devastating as producing a flop.

◉ How about...

... making a habit, when you see a successful product or marketing activity, of asking yourself whether you would have gone along with it, in advance? Would you have had the intuition to approve the investment without a prior test?

If you are being honest with yourself, you will answer "no" quite often which, in turn, makes it interesting to work out for yourself why not. Realising when one's own judgement is not enough and where it falls down can only help improve it over time. But it will still always be advisable to check unless you are virtually 100% sure.

Why you should know and use the "Fact Hooks" in your product category – or, even better, invent your own

"Consumers can be pretty silly, can't they? We spent huge sums of money on improving every aspect of our computers and now they really are amongst the best on the market. Yesterday, I spent some time in a store to see how they were being received and what did most of the people want to know? How many Gigahertz the processor has and that's about it. Yet there's loads of things that determine how fast a computer is. There's... "

It's not reasonable to expect consumers to be experts in all of the categories they buy products from. Yes, they can attain a certain level of knowledge about products that are particularly important to them but the simple fact is that most consumers simply don't know very much about the products they are buying. What is more, they have neither the time nor the inclination to learn any more about them.

This doesn't mean that consumers are prepared to buy products and services blindly, however. Instead, they look for a short cut to a minimum level of knowledge which is why they tend to orientate themselves to one or two key details about a product category whenever they can. These "Fact Hooks" (for want of a better name) such as the GHz performance of the computer above become, after a while, the benchmark for a quality product that every manufacturer has to be measured against – whether there is any validity to this assessment or not.

Such "Fact Hooks" vary greatly from one category to the next and can take many forms, although strangely such "knowledge," is rarely very accurate. Looking at further examples, in consumers' eyes:

- **Good honey is "kaltgeschleudert".** Even though few people know what this means, and despite the expression being fairly redundant because honey is almost always extracted at about hive temperature, brands that don't proclaim that their honey is "kaltgeschleudert" are simply inferior in consumers' eyes and will only be bought at a very low price, if at all.

- **Cakes taste better if they are made to an original recipe (preferably from someone's grandmother).** Quite why 80-year old recipes should be better than those that take modern nutrition theories into account need not be understood but a cake factory would be remiss not to use such a descriptor, where they can – grandmothers are, after all, experts in emulsifying techniques and E numbers. Similarly, an "original Italian recipe" can help sell German-made pizzas in Holland, no matter how odd this logic actually is.

- **The more pixels a digital camera has, the better it is.** Even though only those consumers blowing up their pictures to mega-poster proportions will ever notice any difference once the 4 Million pixel level has been reached, and despite the quality of the lens making a far bigger difference to the pictures they take, the number of pixels a digital camera offers is the measure consumers go by. Any manufacturer who offers a range of digital cameras is forced to correlate pixel numbers and price or risk confusion.

Given that consumers make many decisions by using such "Fact Hooks", manufacturers can only be encouraged to find them for their categories and use them where they can.

Ideally yours will be the company that actually establishes the "Fact Hook" benchmark just as the cosmetics company did who managed to convince women that **face creams that don't irritate the skin are hypoallergenic** – see earlier.

⊙ How about...

... sitting with your consumers and finding out the "facts" they do know about your category and, in particular, how they tell a good product from an inferior one? Whether they are, in fact, true or not, these insights can be used to gain an advantage over the competition, especially if you manage to give them a name that becomes the "Fact Hook" for the category.

This, by the way, is one of the few exercises where your R&D department should probably be excluded. They will be of little practical help as they know too much to begin with and may even be unknowingly obstructive, when the "facts" inevitably turn out to be oversimplifications or are even just wrong. Do be sure to check the Fact Hooks with R&D and the legal department afterwards, though.

Loving insights – a short summary

You should now know a little more about Consumer Insights and about finding strong ones for your brands, including:

- What insights are, what they are not and why they are so powerful

- Why they are talked about far more than they are used

- The various ways to find them, especially if you look in the right places and keep an open mind

- The need to validate even the most appealing insights

- Their relevance to all aspects of marketing

- How enjoyable it can be to look for and work with them.

While the time seems to have come for Consumer Insights, it may be difficult to develop a sense of urgency to start working with them (more) for your brands, knowing that the idea has been around for almost fifty years - yet there is a good reason to do so sooner rather than later. The ever increasing interest in Consumer Insights amongst brand owners still contrasts markedly to the fairly low level of actual usage in marketing activities – but this is set to change. Right now, there is a window of opportunity for those prepared to get in early and start loving before everyone is at it!

Learning to love insights is good advice for all brands too, regardless of their market position. Market leaders can cement their status by using their hopefully superior knowledge of the consumer to counter any reason their users might find to be unfaithful. Smaller but confident competitors can find new ways of attacking the market leader by taking advantage of unmet needs – real or imagined. And those brands that feel "misunderstood" by consumers and believe their qualities are being unfairly ignored can show just how relevant their product's offer really is.

Consumer Insights – leveraging them

Finding and identifying strong insights is very worthwhile but it's not that easy - and it's not enough, by itself, either. There are far more marketers writing insights dutifully into documents than there are brand activities that reflect them actively – the paradox discussed earlier. It is only when a brand actually does something with the insights they have found, i.e. leverages them, that anything positive can result from the efforts undertaken to find them in the first place.

This middle section looks at the application of insights, at integrating them into the daily work with brands and at ways of ensuring that they don't disappear somehow before making it to market. It's often a very long development path that leads from an initial briefing to actual marketing activities and there are many escape routes for insights to take.

It is usually at this stage, when theory turns into practice, that those not yet convinced of the power of insights begin to suspect that there might be something to the idea after all. Seeing insights integrated into briefings and how this then helps to produce different and better results can make marketers wonder why they haven't been working this way all along.

Why, when writing briefings, working backwards from where you want to be is so dangerous

"I've always found insights to be a bit of an academic exercise. We formulate them in such a way that they lead directly to the product benefit that we're offering, in order to make sure that all parts of a briefing or strategy harmonise with each other. In the end, it makes little difference whether we look at the insight or the strategy when we develop our activities because they are just about the same thing, worded differently. Maybe we should just stick to writing strategies and save ourselves the time!

Considering how well ordered and disciplined many marketers' thinking is, it is sobering to realise that the most common way of writing briefings is by starting in the middle! With the false sense of knowing what they think should be written under the heading "brand benefit," this section is filled out first with the parts of the briefing that come before and after the benefit being written to match the middle.

While this approach certainly can produce briefings free of contradiction, it is fairly abstruse to write Consumer Insights to match a benefit rather than the other way round. A benefit is supposed to be an "answer" to the insight found, rather than the insight being the formulation of a question that leads to a pre-determined benefit. It's a little like deciding that the answer to a quiz question has to be "Bush" and not caring whether the question is about a president or a plant.

You can usually tell when insights have been reverse engineered this way. They read like the body copy in a brochure, lack authenticity and are obviously not really based upon how consumers think and feel. They probably aren't even Consumer Insights at all, simply manufacturer thinking put into quotation marks and dressed up with "I's" and "we's".

Interestingly, there is a reason why deciding on the benefit and then working out the insights backwards doesn't seem particularly wrong to many marketers when they write briefings. Such documents are often seen to consist of a number of empty boxes with questions at the top of each box, which need to be "filled out" in order to get the job done. Viewed this way, it doesn't really matter in which order the boxes are filled out, as long as they are all complete in the end and the content is not contradictory.

This is not a sensible way to write any document, particularly a briefing, as it treats the exercise as a duty rather than an opportunity to refine one's thinking. A better form of briefing can help ensure that this mistake is not made – see the following section.

Why insight-driven linked briefings offer the best chance that insights make it to market – and what such briefings should contain

Good briefings, whether for R&D departments, agencies or other external suppliers of communication, should be treated not as a set of boxes to be filled out in any order you like (see above) but as linked chains of thought that are worked through from start to finish. Quite simply, each new section should be written based upon what has previously been thought through and decided upon.

Most companies' and agencies' standard briefing formats don't take linkage into account at all. Often, they're almost an invitation to the writer to fill them out like a questionnaire, in whatever order they can come up with the right answers. What they should be is more of a guideline to thinking a task through from beginning to end.

Linked, insight-driven briefings offer a better basis to work from for any marketing activity as they offer a better chance that hard-won insights will actually end up in whatever is being developed.

Here is an outline for an insight-driven linked communication briefing together with a brief explanation of what should appear in each section and a fictitious, worked example. Each section refers explicitly to what has gone before, which means the briefing really has to be written from top to bottom to make any sense.

(A blank version of this linked briefing can also be found in Appendix 2, should you wish to try working it yourself.)

A ten-point insight-driven linked communication briefing – complete with explanations and a worked example for "Kleines Wunder."

1. Background information, relevant to the planned creative development

Many people are uncertain what to write in the background section of a briefing: should it be everything that is known about a brand so that even those unfamiliar with it can be enlightened, or just a bare minimum of facts?

The best guideline that can be given is to take the word "relevant" very seriously and then include as much relevant information as is necessary, and as little as possible for the reader to understand the task at hand.

If there is a need for more data, it should be attached in an appendix. It may not actually end up being read but it will prevent the briefing itself becoming so long that it, too, is in danger of being ignored.

Here is a sample background for a brand called Kleines Wunder. This fictitious example will be used throughout this briefing to make things less theoretical.

> *"Kleines Wunder is the leading brand of rice-based ready meals and has been a family favourite for years. It is popular particularly because of the superior taste of the special sauce – contained in the Wundertüte – which is heated separately and then poured over the rice just before serving.*
>
> *Recently, Kleines Wunder has been losing market share to instant brands. These produce a meal that is, objectively, not as tasty or as nutritious as Kleines Wunder but takes only three minutes to prepare instead of 15. These new products also come in a wider variety of flavours such as Thai Chicken and Spicy Chilli.*
>
> *It is planned to add new varieties to the Kleines Wunder range but not venture into ethnic tastes. The brand will also stick to the trusted 15 minute preparation method and stress the quality and tradition that the brand stands for."*

2. Objective(s) of the planned communication, considering the background

Communication is rarely planned without a reason or a goal yet it is quite rare to find objectives formulated precisely. The goal(s) should be framed within the context of the background and should be as clear as possible, should not be open to individual interpretation and, importantly, must be measurable – if results cannot be measured, how will you ever know when and whether the objectives have been achieved?

There should be as few objectives as possible and, if a list is unavoidable, they should be written in order of priority. Just remember that anything that isn't top priority rarely gets done.

> 1. *"Return Kleines Wunder to a 50%+ market share (volume) versus the current level of 45% by year end.*
>
> 2. *Achieve at least a 60% level of rice-based ready meal users who agree with the statement "it is worth taking the necessary extra time and effort to serve my family the "proper food" that is Kleines Wunder" – an increase of 10%, as measured in tracking data.*

3. Target Group for the activities to be developed

The Target Group should contain a brief, demographic description of those consumers that the communication will be trying to influence, psycho-graphic information if relevant (and not simply because it is available) and, ideally, an indication of the behaviour of the Target Group toward the brand and category now.

> *"Town and city mothers with children at home who want to serve good food and have "proper" meals with their families but who are also pressed for time. They have grown up with Kleines Wunder themselves and have a very positive attitude towards the brand – yet they are still attracted to instant alternatives because of the time-saving possibilities."*

4. The Consumer Insight(s) to be leveraged in the communication

In this briefing, the inclusion of Consumer Insights is mandatory – in other formats they are often only optional. The insight chosen should represent the best opportunity for the brand to be relevant to the chosen Target Groups' lives, within the context of the background. (It is called a linked briefing!)

> *"My mother used to serve Kleines Wunder when I was at school – those were the lunches that were always a bit special for us and we all looked forward to them. I still enjoy eating the Wunder now, when I make it for my kids. I have to admit, though, that those new instant rice meals you can buy don't taste bad either and fill the kids up just as much. And, as they're so fast to prepare, it means I can get on with doing other things."*

5. The benefit that "answers" the Consumer Insights identified

The benefit that the brand offers should provide consumers with an answer to the need or desire that has been highlighted in the Consumer Insight. The benefit is very likely to be a combination of both rational and emotional/psychological elements, as few insights will be purely one or the other.

> *"Convince the Target Group that only Kleines Wunder makes family lunchtimes that little bit special and that it's worth taking the little extra time to get that unique taste and experience."*

6. The reason why the benefit can be promised

Here, the explanation of how the brand can deliver the benefit it is promising should be included and nothing else. Only facts that should be part of the final communication should appear here.

> *"Kleines Wunder is the only one with the Wundertüte – the pour-over sauce with the secret recipe that everyone loves."*

7. The IdAM* – the Insight-driven Advertising Message

The IdAM, the Insight-driven Advertising Message, is a proprietary name for a summary, in one chain of thought, of the Consumer Insight and the brand's benefit which answers it (along with the reason why, if it is mandatory that this appears in the communication).

The IdAM is the heart of this linked briefing and contains everything that consumers should understand about the brand having seen the communication to be developed.

The discipline of formulating an IdAM is a good test of the integrity of thought in a briefing, too. If it's not possible to compact these important elements this way into just one chain of thought then there are still issues with the briefing that will delay development.

> *"For family lunches that everyone will look forward to, it's worth taking that little extra time to make the unique taste of Kleines Wunder – the only one with the Wundertüte."*

8. Tonality and guidelines

Mea Culpa – this section and the two that follow are not actually linked to what has gone before. This section lets those who are working on the briefing know how a brand is seen or should be seen by consumers and what can and cannot be done in its name.

> *"Kleines Wunder stands for timeless, effortless enjoyment of family life, every day."*

9. Timing

It should go without saying that a briefing should make it clear to everyone exactly how much time is available for each development stage. Ideally, there will be enough time to do a good job, too.

10. Sign-offs.

Not many companies do so, but it is a good idea to insist that everyone who has to sign off on the communication activities themselves, sign off on the briefing, too, before development starts. For some reason, having to commit a signature to paper provides the impetus for many people to voice their concerns at the beginning of the process, rather than at the end.

 * The IdAM discipline was developed by Anke Worringen of Konzeptbüro and myself as an effective tool to increase the probability that insights, once found, actually end up being dramatised in communication and not just written down and forgotten.

Why some creative departments won't thank you for insisting on leveraging insights

"Most briefings that land on my desk are a waste of paper – often a lot of paper, as well. They're full of tons of information that I can't use and yet they still don't contain the very thing I need to make good advertising – the main message reduced to a simple but interesting thought. If there are any Consumer Insights included, they rarely have much to do with the rest of the briefing, it's more like 'here's something that might be helpful' but usually it isn't, just something else that someone wants to see mentioned in the advertising somewhere."

The creative development process, as has been well documented, is neither linear nor easy to plan. No matter how hard it tries, a creative team cannot guarantee having a great idea by tomorrow evening or even next week, although they should be able to guarantee having some workable ideas by then. Sometimes, a great answer comes in a few hours, while it can also happen that even four weeks aren't enough.

As the creative process is already difficult, many people with the word "creative" in their job description try to insist that briefings are as open as possible – especially those creatives with little experience or with their own agenda. The more general the briefing is, they reason, the more room there is to manoeuvre and the greater the chance that a big idea they're going to have will fit the brief.

Encouraged by award-winning advertising that, frequently, finds a new and creative way to convey a generic category message (which may or may not be tied effectively to the brand) they either fight against specific demands on the communication or, more often, simply ignore them.

So adding insights to a creative brief and demanding that they be taken seriously and reflected in the communication is not a recipe for winning popularity in the creative department. In fact, the ability to produce great communication based on such briefings separates the few true commercial experts from the advertising artists.

As a brand owner, having decided that leveraging a strong insight is the best route to take and having painstakingly found the right one, it makes no sense to allow it to slip away again because a creative team is either unwilling or unable to work this way. It is probably easier to find another, more flexible creative team than it is to find another strong insight.

◉ How about…

… trying to convince your creative partners that just because you are giving them a narrow brief, you aren't closed to unusual creative ideas, if they are on brief?

As it happens, as long as creative work does get across the IdAM (the Insight- driven Advertising Message, see Page 59) then it can be very new and unusual and still lead to success. This is because a brand need no longer worry about adhering to the norms in communication for the category – if the IdAM is correct and the communication has no other obvious problems of taste or understanding, then it will most probably work.

One good piece of advice for anyone working with creative teams is to make a habit of collecting communication you like and showing and discussing it with them on occasion. A few, insight-driven, prize-winning TV spots for VW that you show them will work wonders for your relationship.

Why insight-driven local brand names can be an advantage over harmonised international competition

"I work for a multinational and they are great believers in the power of a brand name. They always look for names that are emotionally descriptive of the product they are selling and spend a small fortune finding out the best ones. They're pretty good at it, too. Unfortunately, they believe just as strongly in global harmonisation, so the great names they find for the US market get used here in Germany as well. Not only don't we profit from such names, consumers can't even understand them half the time."

The power of a strong brand name is well documented although, interestingly, many of the brands we have known for years would not get the thumbs-up from most marketing departments nowadays. Would you, for example, honestly put your money on a new food range called Dr. Oetker or sweets bearing the name Haribo?

Ignoring those companies that name their products after the owners (still common amongst retailers, electronics and computer companies) many spend an impressive amount of time and money looking for just the right brand name – something that will add to the pure product description, rather than just exist alongside it.

I have a particular liking for descriptive brand names, where the product's benefits are communicated by the name alone: Hohes C, Nimm 2, Dick und Durstig und Merci are just some classic examples of this approach which is used far too infrequently.

When it comes to names for international application, however, new rules apply and there appear to be two opposing schools of thought.

On the one hand there are companies that plan internationally from the start, purposely looking for names that mean absolutely the same wherever they are used. Given the diversity of languages, this usually leads to the deliberate choice of brand names that have no meaning at all, anywhere.

In order to find such meaningless names, name-generating software is frequently used to write lists of five or six-letter combinations (usually with two vowels, arranged as in xaxxax). These can then be evaluated by different departments and countries. The results – the best known of which include Kevlar and Teflon – are rarely memorable and take relatively long to establish themselves.

More recent international names without any real meaning, such as Yahoo, Google and eBay, are at least easier to remember, although this probably has more to do with their in-your-face web background than international planning from the start.

The opposite approach to finding names for international application is to find the best one for the brand in the country where the product is to be launched and then… well, essentially, ignore the fact that whatever makes the brand name work well in the original country will almost certainly not apply to most other places.

Examples of this approach include Pampers (yes, it has another meaning!), Toys-R-Us, Fairy and Head & Shoulders, all of which had to establish themselves (or not) in non-English-speaking countries without the benefit of consumers knowing why these particular names had been chosen. (It is probably no coincidence that three of these brands come from the same company who, interestingly, are also the strongest supporters of Consumer Insights.)

These two, very different methods of finding brand names to be used identically wherever a product is to be sold leave the door wide open to companies who simply aim to choose the best possible name for each local market no matter how many they operate in. These companies can look for names that take local insights into account without having to worry whether the words chosen mean anything elsewhere – because in other countries the names will also have been based on local insights.

This local approach is almost certain to lead to better results than either the computer-generated meaningless opposition or the imported, foreign brand names that few consumers understand in the way they were originally intended. A good case can also be made that the advantages of having good, local names in each market outweigh the disadvantages that a product faces because it is sold under different names in different countries. These disadvantages can be reduced, too; there are quite a few examples, from ice cream and cheese through to cars and supermarkets, where the use of identical logos and design have made a brand recognisable across borders, despite differences in the local names.

⊙ How about...

... all companies who are concerned only with the local market taking full advantage of this rare opportunity to be better than their powerful multinational competition? How about them basing all of their new brand names on local insights, to make the names stronger?

Currently, a number of local brand owners seem to believe that a foreign name, usually English, will make a brand seem more modern and fashionable than if it had a German name. More often than not, they end up choosing names that are no easier to understand or pronounce than their imported rivals.

A foreign name should only be used where it makes sense in the context of the product. The Trueman's Hot Dogs name, for example, helps the brand position itself in consumers' minds. AOK Clear Action, on the other hand, adds nothing and leaves questions open that a good local name could have answered.

Why the fairly insight free zone of packaging presents a huge opportunity to those companies willing to listen to consumers' real needs

"We have achieved quite significant savings over the years by harmonising our packaging across the whole of Europe. Nowadays, with only four variants, we can cover every single EU market. Of course, this does mean that there are up to seven languages on some products and the printing often has to be quite small. Some of our products are blistered even in countries where the trade does not demand it – but when you see the savings overall, you know it's worth it."

Consumer Reports, a US-based magazine, has started awarding annual "Oysters" to the products that are the most difficult to open. The top prize in the inaugural year went to an electronic product sold by supermarkets that took the testers almost ten minutes to extract from the plastic cage surrounding it and then only by using an industrial cutter. Another award was given to a breakfast cereal that was virtually impossible to open without ripping the bag apart and spilling half the contents on the floor. Such results may have surprised some of the Oyster panel but most consumers would just nod knowingly.

Many manufacturers are actually getting worse in terms of taking Consumer Insights into account when developing their packaging. Driven by an understandable desire to reduce the in-store theft which threatens some shops' existence, to decrease the amount of handling necessary by understaffed stores and to increase their products' visibility on crowded shelves, some companies seem to have forgotten for whom they are making the packs in the first place. Many products are actually even dangerous to open, with estimates of injuries related to packaging exceeding 60,000 annually in the UK alone!

Many packs, especially those from the multinationals, also describe their products in a number of languages in a type size that few consumers can read even if they can find the language they understand. Some also include a declaration of ingredients in English, which would be incomprehensible to almost anyone even if it were printed big enough to read.

Considering that packaging should be the most effective advertising that a brand can indulge in, this is surprising.

Consumers will readily let companies know what they would like to see changed in packaging. Even basic research shows that few of them are happy, for example, with the way they have to open milk cartons, biscuit packs or even butter. High, too, on consumer wish lists are packages which don't break fingernails and the ability to re-seal a product for later use. (Part of the success of mini versions of products in many categories is due as much to the fact that the unused product can be kept fresh for longer than the psychology of small portions such success is usually attributed to.)

⊙ How about...

... more packaging briefings seeking to address specific consumer needs alongside the desire to come up with a more modern and attractive appearance? Including such demands would, of course, preclude knowing what consumers really want from packaging for a specific product.

While demands on various products differ, naturally, the goals then formulated to fit consumer needs would often revolve around the same themes: "the packaging has to be easy to open, the last drops of the product have to be easy to get out and the jar has to be easy to store, too."

New packages developed on the basis of such insights would make consumers far more grateful than "a gradual evolvement of the brand character to match the contemporary mood of the times."

Why insights sometimes have to be hidden to be effective

"We just managed to win a contract where I thought we had no chance at all, even though we are the overall market leader. It's for a product series where, to be quite honest, we've slipped behind the competition a little. Our offer can't have been the best, as one of our newest competitor's products is far faster and less expensive. But, as the buyer told me, off the record, recommending their brand to Management would have given him too much explaining to do, especially if anything went wrong. So we got the order, after all."

All consumers, business or private, can be economical with the truth, especially when being interviewed. And, to be honest, who can blame them? Why should they tell an anonymous busybody why they do what they do when they might not normally tell even their closest friends?

Consumers are not always completely honest with themselves, either. Sometimes, while in their hearts they know why they want to buy a certain product or service, their brains wont let them admit it to themselves. An example helps illustrate this effect.

It's a safe bet that years ago, when babies peed (and more)

into cloth diapers, which had to be washed and ironed only to be peed into again, no mother on earth really liked the task of washing them – there wasn't much to like. So when a world-famous company brought disposable diapers onto the market, the advantages to mothers were apparent at first glance.

Many German mothers were hesitant to change their habits, though, not only because of the additional cost. While the product was a huge improvement to life for the mother herself, what about the baby? Would the baby be happy with disposable diapers too or would he or she be somehow disadvantaged purely for the mother's convenience? A difficult situation for their conscience to resolve.

Reacting to the slower than expected initial acceptance for what was quite obviously a great innovation, the company smartly decided to communicate the advantages that babies rather than the mothers had from the product. "Look, our product actually keeps that nasty, potentially irritating liquid away from your baby – that can only be a good thing, can't it?!" Armed with this baby-friendly logic for buying a product whose immediate egoistic advantages were all too apparent, mothers quickly changed their allegiance. Nowadays only masochists, green eco-mothers and members of fringe religions use cloth diapers.

Sometimes, as this example shows, even when a product is a clear answer to consumer needs, communication has to talk about something else to provide an alibi for purchase, while only implying the answer to the insight that is actually selling the product.

Two further examples show that this is more commonplace than at first glance:

- "Digestifs" are a great aid to digesting a heavy meal (as the name suggests). They're an even better way to consume spirits in alcohol-averse company without being open to disapproval or criticism. The same applies to "healthy" alcoholic drinks with medicinal properties which, by some miracle, often promise a good night's sleep.

- The automated DVD hire machines sprouting up everywhere are a convenient way to have 24-hour access to film entertainment. The added attraction of the anonymity that a dehumanised DVD hire system offers is never mentioned – but the films on offer demonstrate the real attraction for many customers. A similar mechanism, many years ago, helped the magazine National Geographic in the US extend its readership considerably.

◉ How about...

... looking at more products and services this way, to determine whether there are additional reasons for their being bought that consumers aren't talking about? Whilst the exercise is valid for any category it can be particularly helpful for smaller brands in crowded markets where the main category benefits are already well served.

Some of the most fruitful areas to look for unspoken reasons for use are products that are believed generally to have a negative side, a criterion which covers quite a spectrum. Anything alcoholic, sweet or artificial, for example, would qualify. Maybe there is mileage in making health drinks on a beer basis, chocolate being sold indirectly for its calming effect or a coffee brand implying it is the drug of choice to start the day with.

A checklist for evaluating advertising that recognises the role of insights

"Meetings with my advertising agency are one of my favourites but I find the sessions where new creative work is presented really stressful. The creatives always sell their ideas hard and seem to take it personally if I don't like them. Sometimes, even though I can sense that an idea is not quite right, I can't put my finger on what it is that is worrying me. But if you realise after the meeting and then bring it up, they're always upset. "We should have discussed this when everyone was there," they always say."

Unless you are involved in evaluating creative work almost every day, you are unlikely to be an expert at it. Separating a creative idea from everything surrounding it and being able to assess the different components is never easy. Even if you are used to being exposed to new ideas and their enthusiastic creators, a high level of thought and consideration is still required.

To avoid being dazzled by those presenting the ideas or indeed, missing something really good in an idea that has been presented badly, it makes sense to refer to a checklist when assessing creative work. Whether your personal checklist is written down or committed to memory, you are well advised to refer to one – particularly this one.

As none of the checklists for evaluating creative work that I have seen gives leveraging insights a sufficiently high priority, here is one that does.

These are the ten (!) questions that should be going through your mind when seeing any creative idea that you have to give an opinion on, with the leveraging insights mentality built in where ever it makes sense.

Ten questions to help you evaluate creative work – especially new creative work

1. Does the work contain a strong creative idea?

Good communication doesn't just talk about a brand and its benefits; it places them in a context, which helps consumers remember what is being offered. The strongest advertising ideas dramatise a product's benefit in such a way that the Target Group can relate to it easily. And, as we have seen, the easiest way for consumers to relate to an idea is to leverage the role that the product plays in their lives.

Ask yourself:
Can consumers relate to the product as it is dramatised here?

2. Does the advertising match the briefing and strategy properly?

A lot of thought and possibly research will have gone into the briefing process, so creative work that doesn't meet the brief should not really be considered, no matter how attractive the creative idea is. If you have included an insight in the briefing (and why wouldn't you?) then it should be there in the creative idea, either explicitly or implicitly. The benefit dramatised should be the "answer" to that insight.

Ask yourself:
Will consumers be able to take out exactly the same message we formulated in the briefing?

3. Is the advertising likeable? Will other people like it, too?

Most marketers agree that, given a choice, consumers don't buy brands they don't like. Obviously, likeable advertising helps a brand to be liked, too, while advertising that isn't attractive will rarely produce the results that are hoped for.

In evaluating creative work, you have to be very honest because if you don't like something, the chances are pretty high that others won't like it either. This is especially true for humour – if you don't find an idea funny, why would anyone else?

Ask yourself:
Would I like my brand after seeing this creative work?

4. Is the advertising honest and believable?

People don't respect brands that don't tell the truth any more than they respect people who don't. Yet it isn't always that simple to decide what is the right thing to do in some cases. Many claims made about brands are actually true but consumers find them hard to believe so, rather then fight an uphill battle, it is best to avoid them. Other claims are believable for consumers although there is little basis for making them – here, you must decide for yourself (and with your lawyers) whether you wish to make such claims anyway. The best advertising, of course, is both honest and believable.

Ask yourself:
Will the Target Group believe the message as communicated here?

5. Does the advertising match the personality of the brand?

Just like people, brands have personalities, some stronger than others. Once established, they are very difficult to change. When a person or a brand suddenly starts acting differently, the natural reaction is often one of irritation, even mistrust. Once a brand has established a personality, changes to it should only be made gradually even if another image would be preferable.

Ask yourself:
Does this creative work really suit my brand?

6. Does the advertising avoid a heavy hand?

The discipline of expressing precise thoughts in very limited space or time can lead to wooden, fact-filled, overly serious results if you're not careful. Yet virtually any product will profit from advertising that takes a lighter, more positive approach. This doesn't mean communication must be funny, although it can help, but creative ideas should avoid being the opposite of entertaining.

Interestingly, when leveraging strong insights that address both a rational and an emotional component, it is easy to avoid being too heavy-handed because the advertising has to work on a more personal level than most.

Ask yourself:
Does this communication have a light, positive touch?

7. Is it different enough from other ideas that spring to mind?

It can be a comfortable feeling when communication seems familiar to you the first time you see it – it's easy to understand and you know how to react to it. However, unless you are sure that the Target Group does not know the advertising it is similar to, beware of interpreting that comfortable feeling as a good sign.

Unoriginal ideas are rarely big winners, although they can be acceptable safe bets, and are rarely the best thing that a brand could be investing in.

Ask yourself:
What is original in this idea?

8. Is the communication good all the way through?

Many creative ideas are built around one small gem. While finding something really likeable in a creative idea gives you a good feeling, it's not enough by itself. A good payoff doesn't save a routine film, an excellent navigation tool won't help an otherwise lacklustre website and a strong key visual will be diluted by a mediocre headline.

Creative ideas, like the best meals, need to be good from start to finish, meaning both the big ideas and the details have to be just right. Consumers see communication many times and the more they see it, the more they notice.

Ask yourself:
Are the details as strong as the creative idea itself?

9. Is the agency doing it for you or for themselves?

The communications industry is highly competitive and the advertising you run reflects on your agency's reputation, too. For reasons that only the industry itself understands, good reputations are built more by prize-winning efforts (regardless of whether they achieved their goal) than by effective advertising that does its job.

Ideas will occasionally be presented that are designed to do more for the agency than for the brand that's paying for the advertising. While it is in your interest that your agency has a strong reputation, it certainly shouldn't be built at your brand's expense, so beware. One hint – whenever an agency offers to pay for a production itself: start worrying!

Ask yourself:
Who will profit most from this communication?

10. Is the advertising really good enough?

Once you've evaluated the idea, found the agreed insight and benefit and identified the creative work's strengths and weaknesses, you should still ask yourself two last, linked questions. Is the advertising you have seen as good as you had hoped it would be and do you believe it could be better?

It is less difficult than many people think to praise an agency yet still ask them to try to improve on their own work. Good agencies will, in fact, respect your honesty and increase their efforts as a result.

Ask yourself:
Is the advertising as good as I had hoped it would be? Could it be even better?

Leveraging Insights – a short summary

You should now know more about working with Consumer Insights and the advantages of applying them to your brands, including:

- The importance of adhering to insights, once they have been found, and leveraging them ruthlessly

- The need for documents to be written around insights rather than simply include them

- Why insight-driven creative work is more likely to be effective but less likely to win prizes

- How applying insights can improve virtually all aspects of marketing.

Hopefully, you should now also be in a position to start working differently with your brands. If the company you work for has a healthy culture of written briefings (and if you aren't you should be introducing one right away) then this is probably the best place to start leveraging insights actively. Producing insight-driven briefings requires an investment only of time, energy and patience and can lead to fruitful discussions and the famous A-ha effect amongst team members without incurring direct costs. For those working in less formal environments, developing some insight-based activities as an exercise may be the best way to prove the point both to others and yourself.

One of the barriers you are likely to encounter, if you do try to start leveraging insights more, is the feeling amongst some of those you work with that they are not being asked to do anything new. This can happen because the terminology of Consumer Insights is so familiar that it is possible for them to believe that they have been doing more with insights than they really have. Yet familiarity with the phrase says nothing about whether insights have been leveraged actively or not.

The best demonstration for those team members in doubt is simply to ask them to list all of their insight-based marketing activities from the last year. It will probably be a very short list but clear proof of the difference between theory and practice.

Consumer Insights – learning from them

Once you start thinking in terms of insights and what can be achieved when leveraging them actively you begin, automatically, to look for them in areas beyond those directly connected with your brands. There's a clear advantage in doing so, too, as insights used in one context can often provide ideas that are useful in a modified form elsewhere. After all, while the products and services might change, the same consumers pop up across a whole variety of categories.

This final section looks at insights in various contexts (hopefully encouraging this cross-pollination of ideas between categories), argues that an insight approach can help explain most consumer behaviour and even shows that insights can explain why markets develop as they do. The topics covered are fairly wide-ranging but by no means exhaustive but, together, do qualify for the collective title of "learning from insights". Admittedly, it was also difficult to resist the attraction of alliteration.

Why leveraging insights is smart, no matter how fragmented markets may appear

"We are slowly approaching a time when we will be able to address an individual message to every one of our potential customers. Media can be targeted ever more precisely as there's a TV channel, website and magazine for almost every special interest group. And with the technology and data mining capabilities the dialogue marketing companies have access to, we can personalise our mail to a degree that wasn't possible even a few years ago. Soon I don' t think we'll need mass media at all."

It is refreshing to see people in industry being euphoric about something for a change but this unusual display of emotion comes at a price. Misunderstandings about mass media and the increasing number of alternative options available have been the basis for many dubious prognoses about the future of marketing and communication. These misunderstandings, combined with the widespread belief that members of society are all becoming more individual, have lead to articles proclaiming the end of mass messages, the need to re-write all communication rules and similar, misguided ideas.

The success of mass media as a commercial communication vehicle has never been the consequence of there being nothing more individual available. Mass media work effectively in marketing because they are extremely cost efficient both in their development (a factor that is often overlooked) and in their application. Mass media will continue to be cost effective as long as large groups of "the masses" can be reached with the same message. The real question, then, is how much of a danger for mass messages is the proclaimed individualisation of society?

Confusion arises whenever the subject of increased individuality is brought up. While it is doubtlessly true that one particular person's combination of favourite food, most hated sport, shoe size, sexual preferences and opinions on the latest reality TV show is probably unique, this uniqueness does not mean that the person has to be addressed individually whatever the reason to communicate with him or her is. Usually, no matter how different individuals' profiles are, there are only a handful of ways to get through to them on any particular subject.

Let's take the example of Pay TV and its potential subscribers, i.e. the vast majority of the population who have not yet decided to pay extra every month for more channels and additional content. While there are a whole number of reasons that each of these people might give for not taking out a subscription, the following five barriers to purchase would doubtlessly cover at least 80% of potential buyers:

- They don't watch much television and are happy with what they can already receive
- They can't afford to pay more for their TV consumption
- They are not convinced that the extra channels are worth the extra cost
- They would like to subscribe but have trouble justifying the extra expense to themselves and/or their family
- They fear they will end up spending even more time in front of the TV.

Faced with the task of increasing subscription numbers (and assuming these barriers to purchase are correct) those responsible for marketing Pay TV do not have to worry about how individual their prospective customers are when it comes to anything else; for their purposes the insight areas that can be addressed are few and clear.

As the first two barriers to purchase cannot be broken down by argumentation, there are just three left where finding the exact counterargument should produce results. The last one, for example, might well be reduced by encouraging people to spend the same amount of time watching TV but using this time more intelligently with the choice and quality that Pay TV offers them.

With only three pieces of communication, each leveraging one of the last three insights, it would be possible to have a perfect mass media campaign – suitable for all potential Pay TV customers. And this campaign could run while the colour of underwear the Target Group favours is conveniently being ignored.

⊙ How about...

... introducing a discipline to your marketing department that promotes looking for similarities amongst potential customers rather than differences – and then taking only those similarities into account that are relevant to what you are trying to do?

As obvious as this may sound, it is not rare to find product managers looking for "special messages for sports fans because they lead more active lifestyles," or "the right message for the web generation who take in their information differently". Of course, the medium affects how the message is conveyed but it has no automatic effect on the message itself. If there is no reason to vary what is to be communicated then mass media should always remain the top option if budgets allow.

Also, why not introduce total cost comparisons when comparing plans for marketing activities? Insist that cost estimates for all plans include theoretical charges for the many hours necessary for developing the activities, even if they do not usually appear in the budget. Your team will soon realise that the total time and effort needed to put on "the greatest skate night that Hannover has ever seen" is, in reality, more than double the official budget for the occasion. Knowing this, they should begin to appreciate that using mass media is not quite as expensive per contact as it is frequently made out to be.

Why saturated markets are often not saturated at all

"We don't invest much in our brand, even though we're the market leader. In fact, we don't invest much because we're the market leader! We have a huge share of the market, the rest is split up among cheaper brands and private labels and the market itself isn't growing any more. Any money we invest in marketing isn't spent very wisely as the payout is too small, so we keep budgets to an absolute minimum."

Marketers are always making claims about the special nature of the markets they operate in and they often appear, at first glance, to be convincing. Once you've heard the same claims being made about very different markets, however, you have a right to be just a little sceptical.

"We're in a low interest category", for example, is claimed by at least half of the marketing teams in the country and occasionally it will even be true. Often, though, supposed low interest is used more as an excuse not to be very active with a brand rather than being an objective assessment of what the product in question means to consumers' lives. If the right triggers are found, consumers' interest can be aroused for almost any product, whether it be car tyres, cornflakes or coffee filters.

Another, frequently heard claim is that a brand is competing in a saturated market. While again this can be true, such claims should never be accepted at face value without closer examination.

Here are some examples where looking further a field makes claims of market saturation hard to accept.

- **Disposable diapers**. In Germany, few parents use cloth diapers any more and the number of babies born is decreasing, as we know. Short of encouraging mothers to use diapers until a baby is older, surely there isn't much that can be done to increase turnover. There are not many alternative uses for the product so surely this market is saturated.
  Maybe. Yet there are countries, such as Japan, where diapers are changed far more often per day than they are here in Germany. If insights into this more frequent usage could be identified (apparently the result of changing them at fixed points in the day, rather than waiting until the diapers are full), then this knowledge could be applied here too and perhaps there would be more growth to be had after all.

- **Plasters.** The market for plasters would appear to be limited by the amount of cuts and bruises that people acquire. Short of encouraging dangerous behaviour or self-mutilation, surely this market is also saturated as long as the population is stable.
  Unlikely. You only have to travel as far as Holland to find a country where the per capita usage of plasters is far higher than here. As it is unlikely that the Dutch are particularly clumsy (although many of them are pretty tall), a good place to learn what might make German consumers use plasters more often is just a few kilometres west of Düsseldorf.

- **Bottled water.** Germany has one of the safest and most hygienic supplies of drinking water of any country in the world – yet it also has the highest level of bottled water consumption anywhere!
  Water bottlers in any country would be well advised to find

out why such cost-conscious consumers are prepared to buy and carry home heavy crates of the one product they actually have almost free on tap in their homes. Again, transferring such learnings to their own country should prevent any claims of market saturation being made there.

It should be possible to increase the usage frequency of most products, even in supposedly saturated markets, if you can only find out how to make the product relevant in a new way by leveraging new insights.

Coca Cola demonstrated this perfectly in the US when it started promoting its unique mix of syrup and water as an appropriate(!) breakfast drink. This was a successful move, apparently appealing to those who found there to be too little sugar in their high calorie cereal and making instant coffee too time-consuming.

Similarly, Kellogg's found that suggesting their cornflakes as an evening snack was a habit adopted by consumers who were always looking for something substantial that would be ready to consume in seconds.

If the market leader in any category were forced to fulfil certain duties, then surely one of them would have to be a continual search for insights that would lead to an increase in usage frequency for the category. An expanding category is far preferable for all competitors than a situation where everyone is engaged in a nil-sum fight for market share in what is supposedly a saturated market.

◉ How about...

... re-thinking the possibilities of increasing usage frequency in your categories by asking yourselves what would have to happen for consumers of your product to use twice as much as they do now? What would they have to think about and do with the product that they aren't now? Once you get past the joke answers, you should find that some suggestions make more sense than they first appear to and are worth investigating further.

Consumers are also a good source of ideas for additional uses of products as they are very inventive at solving any problems they might have. (The most recorded uses for a product I ever saw were over 50 for Rei in der Tube – none of which had anything to do with washing clothes on holiday.) If these uses, once known, are widely applicable, then a company can make them "official" and increase overall usage frequency as a result.

One recent example of consumer habits being leveraged successfully in marketing activities has been the promotion of baby food to adults who are interested in comforting and nutritious food in small, easy-to-eat portions. By the way, the apple puree tastes particularly good when mixed into white Greek yoghurt!

Why it will always be difficult to align consumers' and suppliers' interests for certain products and services

"If there's something I really don't like it's when companies claim to be "there just for you" or "at your service twenty-four hours a day" – and then they're not much help at all. When you do contact them, all you get is a call centre and a friendly but uninformed person on the other end of the phone. Afterwards, you usually know no more than you did before. Would it really cost them that much more to be as helpful as they claim to be?"

On my very first day at university, studying for a Business Studies degree, the accountancy lecturer let us in on what he called the most important secret for a successful business: "Buy things as cheaply as possible and sell them for more than you bought them. Everything else you will learn here is a variation on this principle."

This basic yet smart advice, which a whole number of companies seem to have forgotten, is also the source of much of the built-in tension between businesses and their clients. Generally speaking, companies should try to buy everything for as little as possible and sell their products or services with the highest margin the market will allow. The ensuing conflict of interest between supplier and purchaser is usually resolved to a reasonable degree by a competitive marketplace and the notion of a "fair price" – but it never quite goes away.

There are other conflicts of interest between the two sides of a sale that can also never be resolved satisfactorily. Some examples will help illustrate this:

- Plane passengers are happiest when there are empty seats next to them: they don't have to spend time far too close to someone they'd normally stay a mile away from, and they can spread out. For the airline, though, every empty seat is a lost opportunity which is why seats will be sold for next to nothing before they are flown empty.

- Mobile phone companies use tempting offers to tie in their customers to their services for as long as possible. While finding the offers attractive, potential consumers have little interest in long-term contracts, especially having learned that in two years time the fair price they are agreeing to will be overly expensive.

- Consumers prefer their products as fresh as possible. Housewives buying dairy produce, for example, usually compare the sell-by dates and take the newest one – even though there are others which are still well within acceptable limits. If the retailer is unable to sell these older products in time then goods have to be destroyed which, in a perfect system, would have been consumed to everyone's satisfaction.

It is easy to find more of these customer/supplier conflicts that are not simply price-based. And all of them place a further question mark against the "we are there only for our customers" philosophy that many companies expound.

It should not be surprising to find that consumers are frequently suspicious of such promises which, in turn, should make companies think twice before promising the world.

◉ How about...

... understanding the exact nature of the in-built customer/ supplier conflicts for your brands and trying to use this understanding to deal with it better than your competitors?

Try thinking through the experience of buying and using your brands and ask yourself what could be done objectively to make things better for consumers. Of course, you could also ask your consumers directly.

Once you have a list of possible improvements that would make a difference in consumers' eyes, you can weigh up the benefits and extra costs involved. It might well turn out that a useful competitive advantage could be gained by actually increasing your costs in a way you would normally never have considered doing.

Companies that have done this successfully include the first frozen food manufacturer to portion vegetables such as spinach before freezing them, the suppliers of mobile phone services who first offered built-in upper cost limits, and the breweries who offer their beer in smaller crates that are easier to carry.

Why increased satisfaction with product performance in a category makes insights all the more important

"R&D spent two years improving the performance of our best-selling product. They tweaked the formula so that a significant difference to the old one could be measured, and optimised the colour, fragrance and everything else as well. The new product doesn't cost a cent more to make and the price has been kept the same despite the product now being better. We beat the competition in any test you can do – but it hasn't helped gain us share at all."

One variant that is often forgotten when considering which marketing activities will work best for a brand is how well the brand's category delivers the basic product promise. Imagine that any product or service you can think of is placed somewhere along a performance scale that ranges from "pretty disappointing" right up to "completely satisfying". The results of plotting very different products might look like this:

- At the least satisfactory end, you would find items such as most plumbing services where high prices, long waiting times and the lack of any emotional advantage combine to make an experience no-one wants to repeat.

- Further along, you would encounter disposable diapers (even if it's not the manufacturers' fault that babies don't just pee) and packet soup, which is only as good as powder re-constituted with tap water can be.

- Still further up the satisfaction scale you would find shampoos, all of which perform the basic task of cleansing hair perfectly well but which still have to contend with consumers' latent dissatisfaction at how their hair looks, part of the blame for which they place on their shampoo.

- Close to the most satisfactory end, you'd find coffee filters, which seem always to make coffee successfully whatever they cost, USB sticks, where even the cheapest ones do an adequate job and sugar, which never fails to be sweet.

Considering where the various products are to be found on this scale, one can conclude broadly that the less satisfied consumers are with the performance of a category, the more they are interested in performance improvements that a brand can offer. Even modest advantages versus the rest of the category can make quite a significant difference to overall product satisfaction so just announcing them in communication is often all that needs to be done.

The higher up the satisfaction scale a category can be found, the less significant product improvements are in relative terms. And the closer you get to the completely happy end, the less consumers see any need for products to be improved at all.

A further conclusion here is that the more a category is delivering what it promises, the more the need arises to differentiate a brand in a non-performance related way. It is not enough just to announce product performance or improvements, a brand must also demonstrate that it understands the relevance of that performance to the consumers' lives and show how the brand fits in.

⊙ How about...

... answering the question "How good is my brand's product category at doing what it promises?" and considering the implications for your marketing activities? How important is it that you leverage insights rather than just make announcements?

It is not unlikely that a company will have products in its portfolio in categories at opposite ends of the satisfaction scale. If so, there is no point applying the "standard company way" of marketing to all of a company's products. This common mistake helps explain why some companies who are so brilliant at selling brands of one type fail miserably when they try to sell others at the other end of the scale.

Why you can make a premium version of virtually anything – and possibly should, too

"Our product is made of the highest quality ingredients you can find. We produce it in the most modern and hygienic factory in the country and it has never been beaten in blind tests, not once. There's no way another company could offer a better version of our product and nor could we, to be honest. Of course, we are the most expensive but we're never short of buyers."

As any scientist will tell you, there's only one form of sodium chloride (salt), so the only difference between sea salt and normal salt is the size of the crystals. This can produce a slightly different crunch when sprinkled on food but used for cooking and dissolved, the two become identical. This doesn't stop many cookery experts, however, from insisting that you use only the best sea salt in their recipes – and provides some smart companies with a huge profit margin.

Similarly, the physical difference between the most expensive beer on the market and the budget, own-label version is pretty small yet products at both ends of the spectrum find their fans. And while top-of-the-range cars aren't identical with your average run-around, the far higher margins they generate for manufacturers show how much less consumers will accept for their money, simply to be premium.

In a never-ending desire to show individuality, to demonstrate knowledge about everything imaginable or simply to display good taste, consumers leave themselves wide open to companies willing to offer "better" premium versions of just about anything. As brand marketers, we have to be thankful for this aspect of human nature and, quite frankly, take full advantage of it whenever we can!

There are probably few products or services that cannot be offered at a higher price as long as the premium can be justified. So, in addition to looking at ways of producing products less expensively, every leading manufacturer of branded goods should also be on the look out for opportunities to add perceived, emotional value to their product and charge more for it – even if they are already selling at a premium.

Of course, the best place to start looking for ways to make premium versions of any product is simply to ask consumers what they are missing in their current brands and what would make them even more desirable or exclusive. No matter how insignificant some of the proposed differences might seem, they could be worth considering as long as consumers would be prepared to pay more as a result.

⊙ How about...

... instructing your marketing team to come up with a more premium version of every product you make, even if you don't (yet) really see potential in the market? Get them to think of both "real" product improvements and those that can be sold as such and see what ideas appear.

Companies who engaged in similar exercises found, for example, that the same water can be sold for twice as much if it is filled in brightly coloured bottles and that half as much chocolate can be sold at the same price if it is individually wrapped. If your company can find an equivalent or better premium idea it can both grow profitably and be seen to be innovative at the same time – and what company can resist such a combination?

Why the only marketing activities that should be conducted are those whose path to success can be modelled clearly

"We were really busy last year in marketing. What with classical advertising, our new website, volleyball sponsoring, events in all cities with over 250,000 residents and a special programme for teenagers, our largest brand alone must have been involved in more than 100 activities. Still, it's worth it – we're growing fast."

There have never been so many ways for a brand's marketing budget to be spent than there are nowadays. The combination of tried and tested mass media, new opportunities due to technological advances and a constant stream of media novelties ensures there is an almost endless choice for a brand team to invest its budget in.

As marketing budgets have not expanded with this increase in possibilities – quite the opposite – it would be extremely helpful to know in advance which of the many options is most likely to work. Knowing this would also reduce the danger of budgets being split into too many parts, none of which is large enough to work efficiently.

One interesting discipline, when deciding what to spend a brand's budget on, is to try to model the path from a marketing activity option through to the desired goal. Two simple examples of such "chains of action" should make this clear:

"The Target Group will see our new TV spot and identify with the mother faced with the same issue that she herself is confronted with every week: what can be served at the weekend when the whole family sits down at the dining table and all have different tastes? As our brand has universal appeal for both adults, because of its nutrition and taste, and children, because of its fun value, it solves the issue in the film. Mothers will be encouraged when seeing this to try the brand out for themselves for their own household next weekend."

"Consumers, who have so far refused to use Voice-over-Internet telephone services because they are worried that they will not always be able to phone (just as they sometimes can't get online) will learn from our insert that our VOIP service has a 100% track

*record and will never let them down. They will then take the next
step towards ordering our cut-price phone service by contacting
the call centre whose number features prominently."*

As oversimplified as the above examples might be, they do
both demonstrate the same thing: a clear, causal path from the
activities planned through to the desired goal. And because
these "chains of action" leverage Consumer Insights, which the
brand's benefit can address, both activities are a fairly safe bet
within the marketing portfolio.

Very often, though, it is difficult to construct even such
idealised communication models for activities that are being
planned. Here are two attempts to construct "chains of action"
for the expensive presence of a confectionery brand's logo on a
racing driver's clothes:

*"The Target Group will see repeatedly that a participant in this
high-level sport identifies with a certain brand of confectionery.
Being themselves a fan of the sport, they will be drawn more to
this brand as a result. The next time they buy sweets they will be
far more likely to choose the brand…"* Or perhaps:

*"Consumers who have so far considered our sweets to be a little
boring will see the brand name on the car and the driver and
will immediately associate the highly desirable world of motor
racing with the product, making it highly desirable as well. The
next time…"*

They're not really very convincing, are they? Even with such
optimistic communication models, it is clear that the link from the
activity to the goal is tenuous, at best. There is no real causality
between the marketing activity and the reaction hoped for
because there is no link between the concrete benefit the product
offers and anything that consumers associate with motor racing.

Sponsoring activities like these, some of which are actually
effective, are frequently hard to justify with reasoning as the
path from A to B always contains a number of associative leaps.
Yet they are far from being the worst offenders. I wonder, for
example, who can plot a clear, causal path from mini-posters
over urinals or even product placement in an early evening soap
to any brand goal worth pursuing.

There's a serious point being made here: if planned activities cannot be linked directly from cause to effect, at least in theory, what chance do they have of working in practise? Shouldn't the inclusion of such activities in a marketing plan be then reconsidered completely?

◉ How about…

… making a habit of trying to sketch out the reasoning for the communication models for any activity your brand is planning by writing down such "chains of action"? They don't have to be formulated perfectly, just include all necessary steps.

Generally speaking, the more causal links there are in these "chains of action" and the less associative leaps, the better chances of success the planned activity will have.

You will find that constructing these models is easiest when activities do actually leverage insights actively. This is because a path of reasoning will, automatically, already be in existence.

For those activities where you find it really difficult to plot the path from A to B or where you find the logic itself is unconvincing, perhaps it's time to re-consider whether investments in clear, causal communication models wouldn't be far more effective and efficient.

Why housewives usually leave their supermarket with the same selection of branded products

"Even though our local supermarket is well stocked and always has new things on the shelves, I never really know what to buy. I have my 'usuals' that I put in the trolley almost without thinking about them but then I look for something different to give everyone a change. I try out quite a lot of new products but usually I end up sticking with the ones I've always bought."

Housewives in supermarkets are not to be envied (and it usually still is women who do most of the shopping, making them almost always our main target group). Before they place any item in their trolley, they have to juggle a whole number of considerations, both factual and emotional, in deciding what to buy. With the exception of those basics that are bought almost blindly, every category of product on display has the potential to place the shopper in a situation where conflicting needs and information have to be resolved – and quickly, too.

Take, for example, a mother buying drinks for the family: on the one hand, she is probably aware of the "five teaspoons of sugar in every can" argument against buying most soft drinks but she also knows that the children, given a glass of apple juice or water, usually leave most of it in the glass. There's the price, too: private label orange juice costs only half as much as the premium brand – but do the family really enjoy it as much? They have commented on the different taste before...

Similar inner conflicts have to be resolved by mothers in the supermarket with the ultra-convenient ready meals that save time but contain worrying additives and make her feel somewhat lazy, with the very special offer Schnitzel that comes from an indeterminate source, and with the family's favourite brand of cheese that is high in both saturated fats and price.

It's no wonder, then, that having found an acceptable "solution" to the conflict in a particular product category, housewives tend to stick with it over time – there are plenty of other categories where the conflict is never resolved optimally and one less thing to worry about is most welcome.

The situation described here does not match what marketers traditionally understand by brand loyalty, which tends to be associated with an almost noble attitude towards a brand. It does help explain, however, why consumers are "loyal" to a brand in one product category yet ignore completely products from the same brand in other categories. That's because it's not normally brands themselves that consumers are loyal to but particular products from a brand.

This small but important difference is one that anyone planning an umbrella brand campaign to "profit from synergies" should consider seriously. Increasing the awareness of, and warm feelings towards a brand name, independent of individual products, does not help resolve the conflict situations that the shopper is confronted with in the supermarket. Only product-based communication, preferably based on insights, can do this.

Brand owners are well advised to understand completely the specific conflicts concerning their products with which housewives are confronted. By finding out from consumers not only how a product itself is seen but also about the situation in which it is consumed, a manufacturer will be in a position to try to break down the "loyalty" that consumers are showing for his competitors, too.

⊙ How about...

... companies trying more actively to help consumers deal with these small but frequent conflict situations? There is much to be gained from being the brand (or being seen to be the brand) that understands consumers' lives best.

Many companies, in recent years, have begun to address sensitive issues by changing their policy on transparency. Rather than avoid anything that could show them in a less than optimal light, they are prepared to talk to consumers about virtually any aspect of their products and help alleviate conflict this way.

The bravest of these companies now include uncensored weblogs on their websites, where both praise and criticism are left for all to see. This is a good place to deal with pre-conceived notions or prejudices about a product or service. Of course, taking this option does mean that there has to be nothing major for consumers – or the competition, for that matter – to be critical of. So, in the end, increased transparency should actually lead to there being less, in reality, for consumers to worry about, too.

Why new users of a brand resemble no one more than those who have been using the brand so far – and why it should almost always be this way

"We've been trying for years to reduce the average age of the readers of our magazine. If you compare this month's edition to the one from exactly five years ago, then you'd see we've made huge changes in that time. The themes we cover are much younger, the look is more modern and our style of writing is far punchier. But if I look at the MA, we've managed to reduce the average age of our readers by less than one year in that time."

"Our beer was traditionally the one that the steel workers drank in copious amounts. In a way, it was proof of the beer's high quality, as

the steel workers were very fussy about what they drank. Nowadays, most beer drinkers work in offices, so we've had to try to move more upmarket but we haven't had much success. Even though we've made the bottle design smarter, the beer less bitter and the advertising more worldly. If anything, we're losing our loyal users faster than we are gaining new ones from different social groups. They're all drinking the lifestyle brands."

Alongside the almost omnipresent desire in marketing plans for a brand to grow by attracting new users can be found the wish that these new users should be somehow different to the current ones. Whether they should be younger, more affluent, more urban or more female than the current bunch, most marketers seem fixed on the idea that they should attract people who are in some way different to those that the brand has appealed to so far.

While, just occasionally, aiming to change a user base radically can make sense, in most cases it's neither realistic nor sensible. Most marketers discover that their user profiles hardly change over time unless their product changes completely – once a brand character has been established, it remains stubbornly constant.

The reason for this apparent inertia is that the current users of a brand are not users by accident. Something about the product and the brand character has answered a need in them and they feel comfortable with their choice over time. It follows that those new users who are attracted to the same brand will be attracted for pretty much the same reasons which, in turn, means that the new users will have much in common with the current ones. In other words, it is almost pre-programmed that the user profile of a brand will stay pretty much the same over time.

(It should not be forgotten, by the way, that, in age terms, maintaining a profile for a brand means that new, younger users must constantly be attracted to balance out the natural aging process of current users.)

As it happens, a constant user profile is no bad thing. Continuity is one of the secrets of all big brands, whether in the product itself, its brand character or in those who use the brand. Just think of classic brands such as Maggi, Jacobs or Kellogg's and ask yourself whether their user profiles have changed much in the last five or ten years.

If a brand is looking for growth – and what brand isn't – "more of the same" is a far more sensible approach to gaining new users than looking for those consumers who don't really fit to the brand or vice versa.

⊙ How about...

... using a standard goal in marketing plans that a brand would like to grow by attracting more of exactly the same kind of consumers that the brand already has – and then describing them well?

In addition to being a more realistic approach, this planned consistency might help prevent a brand indulging in activities that don't suit it at all. It should also encourage those working with a brand to find out just what attracted their current users in the first place. Armed with these insights, they can then leverage them to attract more users who are just like them.

Why sex sells sex more than anything else

"You can tell me what you like but the formula never changes. If you want to sell something, just put it next to a picture of a small child or a nice cuddly animal – a puppy usually works well – sit back and wait for things for fly off the shelf. Even better, put it next to a picture of a well built girl in a bikini or a man with his shirt off – that always does the trick."

Considering how often most of us have the opportunity, if we want to, to look at pictures of half-naked people or, preferably, see the real thing, it is amazing to think that there are so many companies who believe that yet another attractive body placed in close proximity to their product will entice people to make a purchase.

While there are not quite as many obvious sex-based attempts to sell things as there used to be, there is still no shortage of barely-dressed skin in advertising and promotion trying to catch our attention. Just within the last weeks I can remember brands blatantly taking this approach to try to sell car accessories (of course), pork for my weekend lunch (!!) and computer hardware, to name just three. Quite why these brands decided to use sex to sell their products is hard to fathom out.

The reason for touching on this issue is not a moral one; if companies want to spend money showing us pictures of attractive people then why should we complain? Far more interesting, in this context, is the question of when it makes sense to use sex to sell products – because obviously it must work, at least some of the time.

Applying the leveraging insights logic to using sex to sell things, it follows that it only makes sense to do so if consumers believe that a certain product or service can actually help them, say, increase their attractiveness to the opposite (or same) sex, improve their success with their partners once they've found them or, at the very least, improve the way they feel about themselves. So what kind of products would come into these categories?

Fashion brands (especially mass-market labels), perfumes, a lot of luxury badge products and, of course, alcohol are areas where sex is never a bad option to sell a brand with – much of the basic motivation to buy many of these products has to do with sexuality.

Yet the insight approach throws no light whatsoever on how sex can possibly be relevant in choosing which set of chrome wheels to buy, in deciding whether or not to barbecue a pound of best fillet (or did I miss something?) or even invest in a particular brand of laser printer.

In fact, until evidence is produced to show that sex has helped sell a product that has absolutely no relationship to naked men or women whatsoever, then we can only conclude that most sex in advertising is doing little more than advertise sex itself. And sex doesn't really seem to be a commodity that is short of customers.

⊙ How about…

… insisting that any proposal to use sex to sell your product is accompanied with a brief rationale of just why it's the best way to go? Is yet another boy-meets-girl story really the optimal way to sell ice cream? (Maybe it is!) Is yet another come-to-bed look the best way to communicate that a particular brand of shirts is now available with a button-down collar?

What anyone involved with deciding on which creative work to use should be aiming for, when confronted with the option of using sex to sell things, is a move away from the standard reaction – a knowing nod and a brief "Oh yes, sex sells". In its place they need to develop a feeling for when employing sex is the right thing to be doing and when it just distracts potential consumers from what the product really has to offer.

Now what was that curvaceous blonde on the poster at the bus stop this morning holding in her hand?

Why it takes only a couple of good leveraged insights per year to keep a company ahead of the competition

"If we're really honest and look back at the end of a year at everything we've done in marketing and sales, then what usually happens is that a handful of activities have worked well for us and made the year and the others just came along for the ride. It's not even always the products or actions that we thought would work that ended up being successful, either. Sometimes I wonder if we really know what we're doing or just happen to be lucky every so often."

One of the less motivating aspects of the "leverage insights whenever you can" mantra is that it is impossible to do it well all of the time. Even with the best of intentions, tools and brains, the resulting concepts, ideas and products will often still be nothing special.

Fortunately, the methodology doesn't have to produce brilliance every time as long as it is used consistently. Even two or three good insight-driven activities or products per year will put a manufacturer way ahead of the game in almost any market you can think of.

The company that found out that consumers hated it when the extras mixed in with their yoghurt were soggy famously went on to develop a package with a second compartment to keep the extras fresh until they were consumed. The company has not looked back since. While not all of their innovations are as smart, they regularly hit the mark with consumers with one or two new products each year and, just as importantly, with minor improvements to existing favourites.

Similarly, a whole new product segment was established by the company that discovered that while consumers know they should be eating fruit regularly, they find it inconvenient to do so – it's messy to prepare and eat. By liquidising a daily ration of fruit, ensuring it was sweet without adding anything else and filling it into small, well-designed bottles, the company discovered a new way to give consumers a tasty drink/snack and make them feel good about themselves at the same time. The company then applied the same principle to other products and Target Groups with positive, if less spectacular results.

As you never really know where the next category-changing idea or, at least, the one that makes the year's figures, is going to come from, it obviously makes sense to spread the risk. The more insight-driven projects you have running, the greater your chances are that some of the ideas will turn out to be winners.

⊙ How about...

... putting aside an afternoon to go through last year's successful activities and trying to work out just why they worked? Forget all the other known factors for success and failure for a while and look at them only from a consumer perspective. Go on, humour me.

Try to work out the insight, say, that explains why the barbecue promotion in hypermarkets was easily the most successful whereas the identical mechanism failed miserably when tied in to the "read more books" initiative. And do try to find more ambitious explanations than "people prefer Bratwurst to Brecht."

It will not always be possible to throw light on the reasons for success this way but I can guarantee you will find out some unexpected pointers that can be applied again this year, too.

Why insights are one of the rare weapons that are effective in the fight against private labels

"There is something almost perverse about our relationship with the trade nowadays. On the one hand we have to have good relationships with them because we need the distribution. On the other hand we have to fight against them, not only for money, as we always have, but with their own rival products, the own labels. Placed side by side on the shelf next to ours, they look almost identical yet cost less than half. And still we have to behave as if nothing was wrong when we meet them."

The combination of decreasing real incomes and increasing uncertainty about the future has helped private labels grow tremendously in Germany in recent years. Having realised their increased potential, the trade has become far more professional in their private label activities, too.

While we still do not yet have the situation in Germany that can be found in the UK, Holland or Switzerland, the supermarket shelves here are not far behind. Private label products are no longer just cheap and cheerful; some are highly innovative and challenging to the major brands.

There are very few effective ways to fight good private labels. The first rule, of course, for manufacturers of leading brands, is never to supply private labels themselves. More realistically, the phrase "at least not at the same level of quality" should be added to this rule as, ironically, most companies need the volume that private labels bring them.

The second rule is to invest heavily in the brand to anchor it in consumers' minds. This is where the insight approach comes into its own as leveraging insights is one of the few weapons available to manufacturers of branded products that private labels cannot copy. Why not?

Leveraging insights on a product level is not an option that is open to retail brands. If the trade does invest in communication for their own label products, then it is almost always on an overall level – the fairly generic benefits of the whole range have to be conveyed. There is little opportunity for a private label brand to highlight individual products and their benefits – and certainly no chance to address individual product insights.

This leaves the field wide open for the leading brands in each product category. Only they can demonstrate their understanding for what a particular product means to consumers and their lives.

◎ How about...

... thinking through this one disadvantage that private labels have when selling their versions of your brand and working out how to capitalise on it? How can your brand demonstrate to consumers that it understands the role that the product plays in their lives?

How, for example, could a major potato crisp brand show that it knows more about the situation in which crisps are consumed and create brand preference versus the private label's offer at half the price? Imagine the company were to find out from mothers that crisps were always being eaten by the family at a speed which the mothers found to be almost frightening? By investing in product ideas such as "Slow Motion crisps, to be eaten in slow motion" or communication ideas such as "the ones they'll take time to savour", the company would have something in its hand that the private label versions simply cannot copy.

Why leveraging insights makes sense for more worthy causes, too

"All everyone seems to think about nowadays is selling things and making money. I know we all want to live well but aren't there more important things in life, too? Wouldn't it be nice if those smart people using their intelligence on fairly trivial matters decided to challenge their brains and achieve something more worthwhile for a change!"

When we think about advertising and communication, it is usually products and services that come to mind first. Yet a considerable proportion of communication isn't trying to make money at all – at least not directly. Political and information campaigns and a range of special interest groups all try to influence the way we think and feel. As it happens, the "leveraging insights" methodology could work just as well for them, too.

One of the first times that I was exposed to communication that was not designed to make money was when the agency I was working for was asked to look at a campaign to try and reduce the spread of AIDS amongst young people. At that time, far less was known about the illness and few people had modified their sexual behaviour accordingly.

Talks with the Target Group were not particularly encouraging. Between the "it won't happen to me" attitude and the "AIDS affects only drug addicts and gays" misinformation, it was difficult to find a good place from which to start trying to influence behaviour.

Then, by chance, we interviewed a man who, on doctor's orders, had just taken an AIDS test and had found out that he was negative. "That was the worst week of my life", he told us. "I didn't know if I was going to live or die and the waiting was just awful. Even though I'm HIV negative, I'm going to be far more careful in future."

Further interviews with those who had taken an AIDS test produced similar findings. The mere act of having to take a test and the thought process that went on in people's heads while waiting for the results almost always led to a change in behaviour – almost as if they had tested positively which, fortunately, none of them did.

We recommended to the ministry responsible for the campaign that they should leverage this insight. Instead of encouraging people who weren't really listening to be more careful, they should introduce a broad programme to make sure anyone potentially endangered should take an AIDS test now – just in case. Such an action would have no down side, either. Those few who were unfortunate enough to find out that they were HIV positive would modify their behaviour and no longer infect others. And, for the vast majority, the effect we had noticed would cause them to reconsider the risks they were exposing themselves to and adjust their behaviour as well.

The staff at the ministry who were responsible for communication were astounded by our suggestion. Even though they had expected nothing like it, they agreed to consider the proposal and, after a week, could find no fault with the logic.

Following internal discussions, however, they decided that although the move was probably right it was neither politically nor logistically acceptable to those who would be seen to be responsible for the campaign. Instead they ran a series of "use a condom" commercials and hoped for the best.

⊙ How about...

... considering what insights can be leveraged, even if your communication goal cannot be measured in terms of market share or off-take? Some charities already do this successfully in their fund-raising campaigns when they try to make those seeing the communication imagine themselves in the position of those the charity is trying to help.

Where I, at least, have rarely seen any insights leveraged is in the vast communication wasteland of mainstream political advertising. While fringe parties are quite good (in communication terms) at leveraging fears about immigration, the future and personal aversions (do you trust a man with a beard?), the main parties rarely express any thoughts from the viewpoint of those they are trying to influence. Considering the size of the budgets available, and the importance of the task, this should at least be worth a try. On the other hand, perhaps it is better if such communication remains fairly ineffective.

Learning from Insights – a short summary

By now you will hopefully have developed an understanding and a feeling for leveraging Consumer Insights whenever there is a desire to influence consumer behaviour.

This includes:

- The importance of aligning consumer and manufacturer interests

- The suitability of leveraging insights in a wide range of situations

- Consumer Insights' role in the expansion of categories

- Inertia in consumer behaviour and the task of changing attitudes

- How leveraging insights can give brands an edge over those competitors who don't.

Consumer logic follows it own rules which are neither strictly rational nor matched to manufacturers' thinking. And regardless of whether this logic is right, objectively, it has to be regarded as "the truth" as far as brand owners are concerned. A certain amount of consumer education is possible but consumers themselves aren't about to change to suit brands' wishes. This leaves companies themselves to choose whether to adapt to the way consumers think or miss opportunities.

For most people, working with insights regularly actually helps improve their intuition which, if we are being idealistic for a minute, can even help them understand overall human behaviour better, too. Getting inside consumers' hearts and minds, even for commercial purposes, is enlightening on many levels and this newly found knowledge accumulates over time.

Making the first steps towards implementing an insight function

If you have bought into the "leverage insights ruthlessly" thinking – and if you haven't by now, I doubt you ever will – then now is the time to add "…wherever possible…" to the phrase and complete the brainwashing exercise!

Of course, insights can be leveraged just occasionally, for the major activities in a brand's life, such as repositioning, a new strategy, communication, etc. While this would certainly be better than never using insights at all, it's actually very difficult to find areas where leveraging insights would not be advantageous – so why wouldn't you do so?

Using insights in a brand's daily life

Let's take a brief look at something that is more commonplace in marketing a brand than a re-positioning or a re-launch – a simple consumer raffle. Planning a raffle is a fairly straightforward activity although there are a number of elements that have to be thought through and put into place well in advance.

Ask yourself which decisions, when planning a raffle, could be influenced positively by knowing more about the consumers' attitude towards them? They include:

- The number of prizes to raffle – is one big prize better or a whole number of small ones?

- The value of those prize(s) – is it the money or the thought that counts?

- The rarity of the prize(s) – are they items that consumers can easily place a monetary value on?

- The relevance of the prize to the category concerned – is a main prize of a car always a good choice?

- How appropriate is it that a raffle is conducted for the brand at all?

The answers to these questions will vary from one product category to another and even between brands within the same category.

Taking a somewhat banal example, it might be just right for one brand of beer to offer a prize of an exclusive premiere of an upcoming blockbuster in a cinema that holds 100 of the winners' friends (and those who would be on the day). The same prize, however, might cause irritation and a negative effect on the image of a rival beer brand if they ran exactly the same raffle.

Consumer insights can be helpful in getting both the big picture and the details right for marketing activities. While you can rely on intuition and experience, it's always helpful to augment both and find out from consumers directly what would work best for them.

The search for insights can't start anew with every new task

Theoretically, knowing what consumers think about planned activities should always help – but if you have to go through the whole insight search and validation process for every step of every marketing activity, you'll never get anything else done. So how can you leverage insights pragmatically on a daily basis?

Most insights about a brand and a category change only slowly over time. This makes it possible to find out specific points once and then just check them every two or three years to make sure they are still applicable. Of course, as there are a whole number of areas that are worth talking to consumers about, it will still be necessary to canvas them on a regular basis.

What is needed, ideally, is a permanent insight function, one that is continually finding out information from consumers and putting it into a central insight data bank that can be accessed whenever questions come up.

Obviously, not every potential question could be covered this way but the majority of issues would be touched upon over time, as the themes in marketing recur regularly. An insight data bank would reduce the need for *ad hoc* insight information to a manageable level.

An insight bank needs a manager

Having seen the advantages of establishing an insight function and data bank, a decision has to be made on the best way to do so for an individual company. The right solution in each case will depend on the number of brands a company owns, their complexity, the sophistication of the competition etc.

Common to most solutions will be the need for an insight manager. This person will preferably not be an ex market researcher but will have a marketing background and be established as high up in the company hierarchy as possible.

This insight manager will be responsible for a number of tasks, including:

- Ensuring the ongoing search for insights is always present in the company's collective consciousness

- Bringing together sales, marketing and market research in the common quest for insights

- Initiating and running the insight data bank and ensuring that it is being used

- Playing an active role in showing the reticent members of staff how insights could be used more

- Documenting the advantages that leveraging insights has brought the company.

Obviously, the insight manager in larger companies will need a support team, too.

For those companies who are unwilling or unable to establish their own insight function, it is also quite feasible to outsource the task. Here, the success of the operation will depend on providing sufficient access for the outside team to both data and the relevant marketing staff.

Monitoring success

As with any other business investment, it only makes sense putting money into activities that will pay out, so success should be monitored.

A reasonable period of time to expect to see the first results in the field from installing an insight function is after about a year. This should be sufficient to allow the first, insight-driven communication to get on air and show some results.

More time will be needed to demonstrate the positive effects on new product development that an insight approach should bring – the exact length of time being dependent on your company's lead times.

If a company has taken the insight approach to heart, major changes across the board should be noticeable to everyone after about two years.

Case study – putting insights to work – Xiu It!

Xiu It! The new brand of chewing gum for adults

The following "case study" isn't really one at all – it is made up and not based on any real situation. This will be immediately apparent as it takes place in a chewing gum market with two equal rivals.

While the situation and "facts" described bear little relation to reality, care has been taken that the case works as a whole. It helps show how an insight-driven approach can work in practice when developing new brands and marketing activities. One advantage of being made up is that the case can be relatively brief, without having to simplify an actual situation to such a degree that it might as well have been made up in the first place.

The case is concerned with the insight-driven development of a new chewing gum brand for adults called Xiu It!

Background:

The chewing gum market has been split fairly equally between two rival companies – Drew Inc. and Florida International – for many years. Following a long period of steady growth, the market has been stagnating, despite a steady stream of new brands being launched. These new brands have usually offered functional benefits in addition to the category basics of "refreshment" and "something to do with your mouth", and are promoted heavily until the next new product comes along.

The rivalry between the two companies to be first on the market with an innovation is intense, although it doesn't take very long before a product launched by one of the two is copied by the other. When Drew Inc. launched *Ultra Sparkle*, a gum with built-in tooth polishing agents, Florida took less than six months to counter with *Bright Lights*, a virtually identical product apart from the taste. It doesn't help that most of the innovations are just marketing inventions rather than applications of new technology.

The situation is not seen positively by either company. "We don't mind the stiff competition at all", said Ralf Stimme, the Marketing Director for Drew, "our real problem is that neither company has been able to expand the market in recent years. We just can't seem to win over certain consumers to using gum at all. Adults, in particular, are chewing gum less and less."

As all good marketing directors do, Stimme decided not simply to accept this situation but to do something about it. He made it a personal goal to win over more adults to the gum cause, with a product that was harder for Florida to copy. He decided to achieve this either by re-inventing an existing product or by developing a new one specifically for the purpose.

The development process started, as always, with the consumer.

Looking for insights:

Stimme's team (with a little outside help, no doubt!) decided to find out why adults were not using gum and what would encourage them to do so. They looked at all of the available research, set up additional, qualitative sessions to generate more specific information and after a few weeks had found out how to proceed.

They soon realised that it doesn't make much sense to try to convince those adults who weren't gum users when they were younger to start chewing now, so identified lapsed users as the main target. Putting together what the team had found out about this particular group, they determined that the three main reasons why adults who might still use gum don't do so any more were:

- They don't believe it is acceptable as they get older to be seen chewing gum – it doesn't fit their overall appearance

- They don't like the image of the gum-chewer – it's not very aspirational

- It has unpleasant side effects! (Not much to be done here!)

Additionally, Stimme's team found out that the three things lapsed gum users missed most about their gum-chewing days were:

- A fresh feeling in the mouth

- The physical act of chewing, which helped them relax

- That using gum helped them concentrate, whatever they were doing.

Based on these findings, a number of insight-based concepts were developed.

Insight-driven concepts

The team combined the insights they had found with the benefits that were being missed and produced verbal, insight-driven product concepts. These were then tested quantitatively for their broad application. One, in particular, was evaluated favourably by almost all respondents – fortunately!

The winning concept read as follows:

Insight	*"When I chew gum it helps me concentrate but I don't feel very comfortable doing so any more. It is difficult to look the way I want to and be taken seriously when I'm chewing, especially when there's quite a lot to chew! I find I'm using gum less and less nowadays, even when I'm not with other people – but I do miss it, particularly when I have to work for long periods of time."*
Benefit	The new, discrete chewing gum from Drew Inc. actually helps you concentrate and improve your memory.
Reason Why	The mini pellets contain a natural, oriental ingredient known for boosting the brain's performance.

Apparently, it would take a new product, rather than the re-positioning of a current brand, to win over these lapsed users.

Brand development

The idea for the product concept had not been pulled out of thin air. The Drew Company really did have an ingredient in their Tokyo subsidiary that could be shown to aid concentration in a way. Apparently, the substance, when mixed into gum and chewed, stimulated the production of insulin, which helps people remember things. The name of the ingredient was too chemical for marketing purposes but the functional benefit could rightly be claimed.

Stimme's team decided that they should use not only the ingredient's functional properties but it's Asian heritage, too, as Asian products were enjoying increasing popularity and were seen to be sophisticated and contemporary.

The team briefed their laboratory and, in turn, their external branding, design and advertising partners on the new project. The aim, for all of them, was to help come up with proposals that, in Stimme's words *"re-invent the gum category for lapsed adult users with an Asian-feeling product that helps those who use it concentrate and improve their memory."*

The various development processes took the usual number of weeks and after many meetings and a number of further tests the whole brand package was ready. It's main ingredients were as follows:

Name

The new product would be called Xiu It! – pronounced "Chew It" – in a pseudo-Asian style. By using this variation of a generic product property, a way had indeed been found to re-invent the gum category for sophisticated, adult consumers. The name, in tests, proved to be unique and memorable.

Packaging

Xiu It! would be sold in small round boxes with an esoteric, vaguely Chinese design in green. They would be rather like peppermint tins, with a sliding dispenser, and designed to slip easily into pockets.

Product

Xiu It! would consist of small, round pieces of light green gum that were smaller than standard gum tablets. They would have a subtle but long-lasting taste, rather like a minty green tea. The product would be claimed to contain "Imori", the new name for the ingredient that stimulates insulin production and helps the memory (derived from an amalgam of the words insulin and memory).

Communication

The benefit of aiding concentration and memory would be in the foreground, supported by the "acquired" Asian heritage. The communication idea would be "Xiu! It over" whenever something needed to be done where concentration and memory were required. Situations chosen in advertising would include those where someone was alone, not only with friends, and the small size of the pack and the pellets would also be emphasised. The fact that the product could be enjoyed discretely in company, too, would also be addressed.

Price

A premium price would be placed on the product as tests showed that it was not only acceptable to the Target Group but also even expected, especially considering the concrete benefit that was being offered and the adult nature of the product.

Final tests

As a last step, the marketing package was tested as a whole. Lapsed gum users responded particularly positively to the benefit being offered, recognised the advantages of having such small tablets and appreciated the Asian imagery, which they could easily relate to.

Small, fine-tuning adjustments were made and then the new insight-driven product and marketing package were ready to be launched.

Next time you have to concentrate, Xiu! It over.

Mirages, E²s, Losers and Safe Bets – the MELS matrix of communication effectiveness

Great creative communication never fails to fascinate me. Even though I've seen thousands of ideas over the years, in various stages of development, an interesting new way of communicating what is often a fairly banal message always draws my admiration.

For me, great creative ideas are fresh, surprising and, above all, relevant – the factor that makes them effective and so difficult to find, too. Brands such as Volkswagen (internationally), Sixt and Nike manage to fulfil all of these criteria consistently but, unfortunately, such companies are rare.

Ideas don't have to be spectacular, though, to be creative; it is equally possible to appreciate the nuances of a well made slice-of-life TV spot, the ingenuity of well made ten-second programme headers and those few websites that manage to be interestingly different without losing their usability.

Personally, I have far less time for creative work that is loud and provokes people just for the sake of it, ideas that dramatise a generic benefit only to be followed by a logo, or even spots that are good the first time but become more irritating with every increased exposure.

There is no objective measure of what constitutes good creative communication, which is why there are so many theories about it. One belief that I vehemently disagree with is that a communication idea can be creative independently of why it is has been created. For me, communication makes sense only within a context and cannot be evaluated on face value.

(This, of course, is the fault with most creative awards: ideas are declared to be winners by judges who can have little idea of why the work was made in the first place – they are judging in a vacuum.)

Creativity and context – the MELS matrix

Put into context, communication ideas should be evaluated in terms of two dimensions: **what** is being said, the part usually covered by the strategy, and **how** it is being said, the creative idea.

By using just these two dimensions it is possible to plot all communication ideas, whatever the medium involved, on a graph and learn about their probable, in-market effectiveness. The resulting MELS matrix also highlights a surprising insight into the interrelationship of the "what" and "how" dimensions themselves.

The x-axis on the MELS matrix is a measure of the strength of **what** is being said. The more the communication message addresses relevant consumer insights (and the stronger the strategy is) the further along the x-axis an idea is plotted.

The y-axis measures the strength of the creative idea – **how** the strategy is executed. The fresher and more interesting the creative idea, within the context of the category, the further up the y-axis the idea is rated.

Obviously, there is a degree of subjectivity involved in both dimensions but the more people involved in making a judgment here, the more likely the results will be representative of the marketplace.

The resulting matrix is then split into four quadrants, labelled Mirages, E²s, Losers and Safe Bets, as follows:

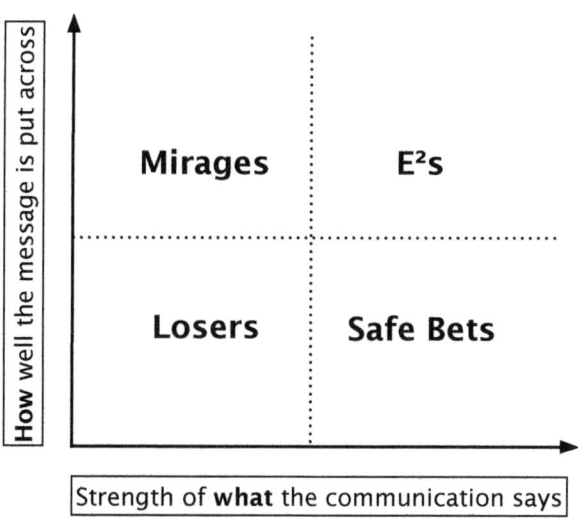

Let's look at each quadrant in turn.

Mirages

Mirages are the communication ideas that polarise our industry the most. They can be loud, provocative, even very funny and frequently win creative prizes, even at Cannes, venue of the most prestigious award ceremony of all. Often they have been developed without the shackles of a strategy and sold to clients who either know no better or just want to be in the limelight.

Mirages have little relevance for consumers, however, as they ignore what consumers are really interested in where the advertised product is concerned. As a result, they are ineffective and usually disappear again after a short time – just like the mirages they are named after.

Losers

Losers' messages are no more relevant to consumers than Mirages and don't even have the charm to be funny or interesting. They are based on generic promises wrapped up in familiar, boring words and pictures. Quite why any manufacturer would choose to use such an approach is difficult to understand yet every TV block, magazine and supermarket demonstrates that there are Losers born every minute – the category is the largest of the four!

Typical Losers are the beer advertisements showing a freshly poured glass with a headline telling you the source of the water it was brewed with, corporate campaigns built around the words "we" and "quality" and radio stations whose only claim to fame is that they play the right mix of music.

Safe Bets

Safe Bets represent the second largest category and polarises the industry almost as much as the Mirages but for different reasons. Safe Bets care mostly about communicating a message to consumers, which has often survived batteries of tests, and, being the winner, provides relevant answers to Consumer Insights. The creative ideas to be found here aren't always too fussy about how they communicate, as long as they are understood and get through. As a result, they often use standard communication formats and are often favoured by the multinational marketing companies.

Safe Bets are disliked by many in the advertising industry. Despite being "not creative" in the eyes of many, they work well and not only because large budgets are often used to support them. This disturbs the idealised belief that only highly creative ideas will sell and seems even to decrease the value of the creative discipline itself in some peoples' eyes.

E^2s

E^2s is the name reserved for that rare breed of communication that is both effective and efficient. Like Safe Bets, E^2s address relevant Consumer Insights, which ensures the communication is effective in the marketplace. And like Mirages, they use new, interesting ideas to communicate their messages, which means they require less money to be seen and understood, making them efficient, too – hence the E^2 name.

E^2s, when they are used, are appreciated by almost anyone in the industry but the fear of producing a Mirage prevents many companies from actually aiming to make one for themselves.

Which quadrants of the MELS matrix produce the best results?

Looking at the four quadrants and reading the definitions, it is clear that only two of the four actually produce positive results at all. The E^2s, which by definition produce the most bang for the buck and the Safe Bets, which may not offer the best return on investment but do achieve their desired goals. Neither the Mirages nor the Losers (no surprise there) actually achieve anything but at least the Mirages provide a few smiles and admirable glances.

The surprising insight about the relationship between the "what" and the "how" to be drawn from the MELS matrix is that it is only when the "what" in the communication is right that the result will work at all. If the message is wrong and doesn't address consumers' needs then even the best creative idea in the world will simply not work. Equally sobering is the realisation that as long as the "what" is right, even a mediocre creative idea will prove to be reasonably effective.

Brand owners who understand the relationship between the

"what" and the "how" automatically spend far more time on the former than the latter and limit the time spent on details such as layout alternatives, flash sizes and whether the man's shirt on the poster has blue or brown stripes.

Appendices

Appendix 1 – Zehn Tipps, um sicher zu stellen, dass Ihre Kommunikationspartner ihre beste Arbeit für Sie machen.

Wenn Sie möchten, dass Ihre Kommunikationspartner mitziehen und die schwer gewonnen Insights zusammen mit Ihnen in Marketingaktivitäten integrieren, dann brauchen Sie ein besonders gutes Verhältnis zu ihnen. Gerade in den letzten Jahren, wo das Angebot an Dienstleistern die Nachfrage um einiges übertrifft, gibt es einige Auftraggeber, die darauf wenig Wert legen. Sie glauben, dass eine permanente Bedrohung mit einem Auftragsentzug ausreicht, um gute Arbeit zu garantieren. So funktioniert das aber nicht.

Es ist nicht schwer für eine schlaue Agentur, einen Auftrag so zu erfüllen, dass es keine Beanstandungen gibt – die Arbeit muss deswegen nicht gut sein.

Auftraggeber, die aber verstehen, dass gute Kommunikation einen großen Hebeleffekt für eine Marke haben kann, möchten das Beste von ihren Partnern bekommen und nicht lediglich das Ausreichende.

Hier sind zehn Tipps, wie Sie die beste Arbeit von Ihren Partnern erhalten – und gleichzeitig eine fruchtbare, langfristige Beziehung aufbauen.

1. Ordentliche schriftliche Briefings verfassen

Wenn ein Auftrag wichtig genug ist, um vergeben zu werden, dann ist er auch wichtig genug, um auf Papier gebracht zu werden. „Ich habe keine Zeit, ein Briefing zu schreiben" ist meistens ein Trugschluss.

Es ist nicht einfach Formalismus, ein geschriebenes Briefing hilft dem Verfasser, seine Gedanken zu ordnen und sicher zu stellen, dass beide Partner das Gleiche verstehen. Verbale Briefings sind eine der Hauptursachen für Missverständnisse und eine Garantie, dass „Jobs, die zu klein sind für ein Briefing" doch übermäßig viel Zeit in Anspruch nehmen.

2. Lösungen nicht vorgeben

Kommunikationsagenturen sind Spezialisten und höchstwahrscheinlich (und hoffentlich) besser in ihrem Fach als ihr Auftraggeber.

Wer anstatt eines richtigen Briefings genaue Lösungen vorgibt und dann darauf besteht, dass seine Vorschläge umgesetzt werden, vergibt völlig die Chance, dass die Spezialisten eine bessere Lösung finden.

3. Einen fairen partnerschaftlichen Umgang an den Tag legen

Agenturen sind natürlich Dienstleister, aber einige Auftraggeber nutzen dieses Verhältnis zu ihren Gunsten aus. Die Partner werden unter Druck gesetzt und wenn sie sich dagegen wehren, notfalls ausgetauscht. Dieses Verhalten führt aber bei Agenturen selten zu guten Arbeitsergebnissen.

Die Leistungsträger einer Agentur sind meistens Mitarbeiter mit einer überdurchschnittlichen Intelligenz und Sensibilität. Sie reagieren schlecht auf einen permanent drohenden Liebesentzug – sie sehen die Absichten dahinter und verlieren die Motivation, ihr Bestes zu geben.

4. Der Lieblingskunde der Agentur werden

In jeder Agentur gibt es Lieblingskunden. Dieser für den Kunden vorteilhafte Status resultiert nicht nur aus einer fairen Zusammenarbeit, sondern auch aus guten kreativen Lösungen, die gemeinsam erarbeitet werden.

Lieblingskunden sind die Auftraggeber, für die jeder gute Kreative und Berater arbeiten möchte. Oft erhalten sie auch mehr Leistung als ihr Etat eigentlich verdient hätte – denn die meisten Mitarbeiter kümmern sich nicht um die Rentabilität eines Etats, sondern strengen sich da an, wo sie emotional am meisten eingebunden sind.

5. Genug Zeit geben, um gute Lösungen entstehen zu lassen

Bei einigen Auftraggebern ist es normal geworden, der Agentur immer nur wenig Zeit zu geben. „Sie können am Wochenende Ideen dazu entwickeln und am Montag Vormittag präsentieren."

Die Einstellung, Arbeit immer unter Zeitdruck zu verlangen, lässt aber außer acht, dass gute Ideen nicht linear entstehen (in etwa zwei pro Stunde), sondern ihre Zeit brauchen, auch um zu reifen. Wer darauf besteht, immer schnell etwas zu sehen, wird nur das Tagesbeste präsentiert bekommen und möglicherweise die Leistung seiner Partner danach bemängeln – „sie haben keine gute Ideen mehr".

6. Eine offene Informationspolitik Ihren Partnern gegenüber verfolgen

Die Angst einiger Auftraggeber, ihren Partnern interne Informationen und Daten zu geben, ist meines Erachtens übertrieben. „Die Mitarbeiter wechseln so oft" wird meistens als Grund angegeben.

Abgesehen davon, dass die Verweildauer von Agenturmitarbeitern sich in den letzten Jahren erhöht hat, war diese Argumentation immer etwas fragwürdig. Die Vorteile, Ihren Partnern Zugang zu allen relevanten Daten zu geben, überwiegen bei weitem das Risiko, dass Ihre Geheimnisse preisgegeben werden. Agenturmitarbeiter sind nicht weniger vertrauenswürdig als die eigenen, die externen Labors und Marktforschungsinstitute, die ebenfalls Zugang zu vertraulichen Daten haben. Und Vertrauen zu schenken bringt enorm viel für ein gutes Verhältnis.

7. Ideen in Rohform anfordern, nicht in „Essig und Öl"

Die zunehmenden Möglichkeiten, Kommunikationsvorschläge in fast perfekter Form anzufertigen und zu präsentieren, führen zu unerwünschten Nebeneffekten, die sich gegenseitig potenzieren.

Die Vorstellungskraft der Auftraggeber scheint nachzulassen („Kannst du mir bitte zeigen, wie das Bild gekontert aussieht?"), also wird immer perfekter präsentiert. Dadurch aber fällt das Hauptaugenmerk der Agenturen immer mehr auf die Ausführung der Ideen und immer weniger auf die Ideen selber. Wer auf Ideen in Rohform besteht – am besten nur Scribbles und keine Fotos, Photoshop Montagen oder Illustrationen – stellt sicher, dass er Ideen sieht und nicht einfach geblendet wird.

8. Lob (und Tadel) verteilen, wo es angebracht ist

Die meisten Präsentationen heute folgen einem ähnlichen Ablauf. Die Kommunikationsagentur zeigt nach einer kurzen Wiederholung der Aufgabe ihre Ideen und der Auftraggeber sagt, was er daran verbessert haben möchte. „Ich muss die Agentur nicht loben, sie machen nur ihren Job", heißt es oft.

Dass Agenturen dafür bezahlt werden, gute Ideen zu liefern, stimmt natürlich, aber es sind nicht Firmen, sondern Menschen, die die Ideen entwickeln. Lob, wenn angebracht, ist die beste Motivation, die es gibt – und kostet lediglich etwas Zeit.

Es gibt aber auch Kunden, die nichts Negatives sagen wollen, um nicht „zu demotivieren". Gute Kreative schätzen es aber schon, wenn verständliche Gründe gegeben werden, etwas nicht zu tun. Ein „Ich mag es einfach nicht" ist dabei wenig hilfreich.

9. Gut bezahlen

Mittlerweile sind wir alle darauf trainiert, alles so günstig es geht einzukaufen. Aber wie in vielen anderen Bereichen ist das Billigste selten das Beste.

Einige Auftraggeber denken nicht daran, dass die Kostenstruktur ihres Kommunikationspartners sehr einfach ist; die Hauptposten sind die Gehälter und weniger Honorar bedeutet entweder weniger oder weniger erfahrene Menschen. Es ist erstaunlich, wie viele Firmen sich einerseits mit den niedrigen Honoraren, die sie bezahlen, schmücken und gleichzeitig sich über den mangelnden Service beschweren. Eine Agentur ist aber letztendlich auch ein Business und kein kluger Agenturmanager liefert auf Dauer mehr als bezahlt wird.

10. Gegenseitige Evaluationsmöglichkeiten implementieren

Die Hitze der Tagesarbeit ist nicht geeignet, um eine objektive Beurteilung der Leistung einer Agentur in all ihren Facetten abzugeben.

Viel besser ist es, sich regelmäßig die Zeit zu nehmen, um nach einem vorher bekannten Beurteilungsmuster die Leistung der Agentur mit dem Agenturmanagement zu diskutieren. Falls es Unstimmigkeiten gibt, können sie so schnell gelöst werden. Es ist immer besser, auch große Probleme gemeinsam zu lösen, als mit einem neuen Partner von Null anzufangen.

Der Beurteilungsprozess funktioniert am besten, wenn die Evaluierung keine Einbahnstrasse ist, sondern ein gegenseitiger Austausch. Für Auftraggeber und Agenturen sollten solche Meetings nicht als lästige Notwendigkeit angesehen werden, sondern als Chance, auch ein Fremdbild über die eigenen Mitarbeiter zu bekommen.

Appendix 2 – A ten-point insight-driven linked communication briefing

1. Background, relevant to the development
2. Objective(s) of the planned communication, considering the background
3. Target Group for the activities to be developed
4. The Consumer Insight(s) to be leveraged in the communication
5. The benefit that "answers" the Consumer Insights identified

6.   The reason why the benefit can be promised
7.   The IdAM – the Insight-driven Advertising Message
8.   Tonality and guidelines
9.   Timing
10.   Sign-offs

Appendix 3 – Ten questions to help you evaluate creative work – especially new creative work

1. Does the work contain a strong creative idea?

Ask yourself:
Can consumers relate to the product as it is dramatised here?

2. Does the advertising match the briefing and strategy properly?

Ask yourself:
Will consumers be able to take out exactly the same message we formulated in the briefing?

3. Is the advertising likeable? Will other people like it too?

Ask yourself:
Would I like my brand after seeing this creative work?

4. Is the advertising honest and believable?

Ask yourself:
Will the Target Group believe the message as communicated here?

5. Does the advertising match the personality of the brand?

Ask yourself:
Does this creative work really suit my brand?

6. Does the advertising avoid a heavy hand?

Ask yourself:
Does this communication have a light, positive touch?

7. Is it different enough from other ideas that spring to mind?

Ask yourself:
What is original in this idea?

8. Is the communication good all the way through?

Ask yourself:
Are the details as strong as the creative idea itself?

9. Is the agency doing it for you or for themselves?

Ask yourself:
Who will profit most from this communication?

10. Is the advertising really good enough?

Ask yourself:
Is the advertising as good as I had hoped it would be?
Could it be even better?

Acknowledgments

Special thanks must be given to Anke Worringen, who provided valuable input for many of the topics covered here and whose understanding of consumers and how they think never fails to astound me.

I am equally grateful to my wife Gabriele Graf-Schoen, without whom the book would never have been completed and who also had to put up with me while it was being written! Even a slim volume takes far more time and effort to write than one would expect.

Lastly, I would like to thank Marie Scheuerlein for taking the trouble to read the whole book four times in order to correct the huge number of grammatical and syntax errors

Any remaining mistakes, omissions, bad ideas, weak examples, etc. that have slipped through are, of course, all down to me.

Comments to the content – positive ones, in particular, are welcome – should be addressed to:

melschoen@insightdriven.de.

Many thanks.